M

Text b...
Re...

...ury Pike

Series Editor Tony Halliday

Berlitz POCKET GUIDE

Mexico

Fourteenth Edition 2005

PHOTOGRAPHY CREDITS
Pete Bennett 29, 34, 110, 146, 147, 151, 196, 201, 219; Chris Coe 112, 114, 115, 117, 118, 216; Corbis 83, 84, 129, 180, 188, 190, 192; Antonio García Collection 26, 30; Glyn Genin 15, 134, 136, 141, 143, 149, 150, 153, 155, 195, 207, 209; Tony Halliday 16, 22, 36, 38, 39, 40, 45, 46, 49, 51, 54, 131, 133, 135, 137, 138, 139, 142, 148, 156, 158–9, 174, 177, 178, 199; Adriano Heitmann 9, 11, 12, 14, 50, 59, 68, 72, 78, 89, 92, 102, 109, 119, 154, 173, 181, 185, 187, 193, 210, 211, 217; Hidden Worlds 198; Claude Huber 43, 57, 71, 124; Mexican Tourist Board 55, 62, 66, 86, 91, 97, 99, 104, 107, 124, 168, 189, 215; Powerstock 94; Schülz 24; Topham/ImageWorks 77, 123, 162, 165, 167; Topham Picturepoint 101, 163, 170, 182, 183 203; Marcus Wilson Smith 18, 32, 47, 53, 61, 65, 74, 75, 79, 80, 88, 120, 125, 127, 161, 204, 221; Alison Wright/Panos Pictures 171

CONTACTING THE EDITORS
Every effort has been made to provide accurate information in this publication, but changes are inevitable. The publisher cannot be responsible for any resulting loss, inconvenience or injury. We would appreciate it if readers would call our attention to any errors or outdated information by contacting Berlitz Publishing, PO Box 910, London SE1 1WE, UK. Email: berlitz@apaguide.co.uk; fax: (44) 20 7403 0290; www.berlitzpublishing.com

Acapulco has 20 beaches, lively nightlife – and the famous cliff divers of Quebrada (see page 117)

The drive to the lovely colonial city of Puebla (page 74) takes you past the active Popocatépetl volcano

Chichén Itzá is the largest and best preserved of all the ancient Mayan cities (page 142)

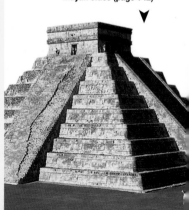

TOP TEN ATTRACTIONS

Wander among the impressive ruins of Monte Albán, in the state of Oaxaca (see page 169)

Get to grips with the Mexican interior on a tour of the colonial 'Silver Cities' (page 83)

Crystal-clear, aquamarine seas lap white sandy beaches along the idyllic Caribbean coast, near Tulum (see page 157)

Fine museums, colonial mansions, a vibrant art scene and great shopping are among Mexico City's charms (page 35)

Mayan traditions thrive around San Cristóbal de las Casas (page 181)

Local colour wherever you go: Carnival in Veracruz (page 186)

The scenery in Copper Canyon is spectacular (page 128)

CONTENTS

Fact Sheets

MEXICO AND THE MEXICANS

In his personal account of the conquest of Mexico in 1519, Bernal Díaz del Castillo described the reaction of the Spaniards when, from the slopes of the snow-capped volcano Popocatépetl, they beheld the valley of Mexico for the first time. Far below was a broad, fertile plain, many miles across, surrounded by steep mountains. Three lakes occupied the valley, with exotic cities on their fringes. Tenochtitlán, the most beautiful of all, lay in the middle of the largest lake, connected to the shore by three elevated causeways and the constant traffic of boats that plied back and forth.

The city was larger than any Spanish city of the time; it had broad canals and brightly coloured pyramids and palaces, with large, colourful banners fluttering in the air. So beautiful and strange was the scene that the Spaniards lacked anything with which to compare it except for the magical kingdoms that populated chivalric novels, the pulp fiction of their time.

A Countryside of Contrasts

The reaction of these Spaniards is something akin to the reactions of present-day visitors to Mexico who come unprepared for the most exotic features of the land and its people, and who often refer to works of fiction when trying to describe their Mexican experiences. Like the conquistadors, modern visitors note the vivid colours – from the warm reds, yellows and oranges of contemporary Mexican architecture to the cool blues and greens of its seacoasts.

Accentuating this brightly coloured palette are the contrasts that Mexico presents. A short ride on horseback in

A modern-day Aztec proudly wears the headdress of his ancestors

Mexico can take the rider from the cool, thin fragrances of high-mountain pine forests to the warm, heady aromas of tropical jungle – never mind what a car ride can do. Walk into a bank and you might be served by an impeccably dressed man in a dark three-piece suit, while in the queue next to you stands a Zapotec Indian woman dressed in an equally impeccable, beautifully worked crimson *huipil* (Indian blouse). Anybody who travels to Mexico will find in the land and its inhabitants much to marvel at.

Striking Geography

Mexico is roughly half the size of Western Europe. It has a lot of coastline, due in part to the two great peninsulas that act as bookends for the country: Baja California in the north-west and the Yucatán in the southeast. If you don't take into account these peninsulas, Mexico has the shape of a cornucopia – wide at its northern border, narrow as it curls to the south and east before it joins Guatemala.

It is a country of mountains, with two long ranges known as the Sierra Madre that stretch from the United States border down the east and west sides of Mexico and converge in the central part, in effect forming a large 'V' that encompasses most of the national territory. The area between the ranges is desert in the north and mainly high tableland in the south. At the bottom of the 'V' and cupped by these mountains is the valley of Mexico that gave Bernal Díaz such a shock, and in which now sits Mexico City, the nation's capital. The area surrounding this and neighbouring valleys is the highest part of the country. Mexico's four tallest mountains (which are all snow-capped volcanoes) can be found here.

The Sierra Madre Occidental is the western mountain range that follows the Pacific coast. Etched into the northern part of these mountains between the city of Chihuahua and the port of Los Mochis are several spectacular canyons known as

Copper Canyon. This is the home of the Tarahumara Indians. In the southern part of the Sierra Madre, sheltered in the valleys, are some of the colonial silver cities. Along the entire western edge of this mountain range lies a narrow coastal plain, except where in some places the Sierra Madre extends all the way to the shore to create mountain-fringed bays of great beauty, such as at Puerto Vallarta.

On the Gulf Coast side of Mexico runs the Sierra Madre Oriental. These mountains receive more rain and are greener than the western range. They have some lovely waterfalls and deep limestone caverns and to their east is a broad coastal plain containing most of the state of Veracruz.

The dormant volcano Iztaccíhuatl is Mexico's third highest mountain

South and east of central Mexico are the Oaxacan highlands, home of the Zapotec and Mixtec Indians, who are famous for their many handicrafts. Mexico gets much narrower as the Pacific coast bends eastwards. Another mountain range, the Sierra Madre del Sur, follows this coast, making it almost entirely mountainous. Here you will find beach resorts like Acapulco, with its famous cliffs, and Ixtapa/ Zihuatanejo.

At one point in eastern Oaxaca the mountains subside and the land between the Gulf of Mexico and the Pacific narrows to only

200km (126 miles) at the Isthmus of Tehuantepec. Beyond Oaxaca is Chiapas, Mexico's southernmost state, a land of mountains and lowland jungles. In the mountains you will find the villages of the highland Maya surrounding the town of San Cristóbal. In the jungles you will find the ruins of Palenque to the north and the ruins of Yaxchilán and Bonampak to the southeast, along the border with Guatemala.

Stretching northeast of Chiapas is the large Yucatán Peninsula – a low, flat land of tropical forests growing in thin soil above a slab of limestone. The land here is honeycombed by underground rivers which on occasion rise to the surface to form perfectly round natural wells called *cenotes*. The peninsula borders the Caribbean on its eastern shore (location of the large resort town of Cancún and the islands of Cozumel and Isla Mujeres) and the Gulf of Mexico to the north and west. In the interior are the ruined Maya cities of Chichén Itzá and Uxmal and the lively colonial city of Mérida.

Multicultural Mix

Today, despite almost five centuries of racial intermixing and acculturation, there are still five million Indians in Mexico who speak their native language, and close to a million of them who don't speak Spanish. The most numerous Indian-language speakers are Nahuatl (the Aztec language), Maya, Mixtec, Zapotec, Tarahumara and Purépecha. In addition, there are many smaller Indian groups in Mexico and about 50 other Indian languages.

The population of Mexico is estimated at 104 million, of whom around 65 million are *mestizo* (of mixed European and Indian blood) and 30 million are Indians. Of the total population, 90 percent are Catholic.

These various Indian cultures have over the centuries exerted a profound influence on the national culture of Mexico. The Indians, however, simply go about doing what they have been doing for centuries. Many are quite comfortable moving about outside their native regions, finding work where they can, but they draw the distinction between themselves and the people they call Mexicans. Yet for some Indians that distinction is blurred when they establish a household outside their native village or marry someone of a different ethnic group. They or their children then gradually

A young *mestiza* in the Juchitan region of Oaxaca state

become *mestizos* ('mixed' Spanish and Indian) and join the vast majority of the Mexican population.

In Mexico, this intermixing of the Spanish and Indian races has been a centuries-long process. More than the mixing of races, it has been a mixing of cultures. The particularly strong Indian influence has given a vitality to the national *mestizo* culture of Mexico that sets it apart from the other Latin American countries where the intermixing has been less thorough, and it allows Mexico to hold its own against cultural encroachments from abroad. Spaniards and South Americans borrow repeatedly from the inventory of slang expressions and word-play of

Mexican Spanish, with its sing-song cadences, its large number of native words and its inventive phrasing. Mexican music has also been widely exported, as have Mexican films and television shows. Mexicans tend to export more culture than they import and as a result the traveller gets the sense that these are people who enjoy who they are.

Religion and Family

One powerful aspect of Mexican culture is its own particular form of Catholicism. Mexicans are active practitioners of their faith. Churches in Mexico don't feel like remnants of a past era; they are much frequented, attracting large crowds. The Mexican form of worship emphasises prayer, penance, pilgrimages, vigils and many festivals, and it owes much to the Indian influence, as can be seen in the celebration of the Day of the Dead. This and other religious festivals are the most outward manifestation of this faith, and they are particularly fascinating to witness.

Family ties are strong, especially among the Indian peoples

Every community has a patron saint who has his or her own feast day, celebrated with much hoopla, and often with rituals that are unique to that town. Add the other favourite saints' feast days, plus the holidays of the civil calendar, and it is clear that Mexicans have many occasions to celebrate.

Religious festivals are just one of several factors that reinforce social cohesion. Another is family. The extended family is highly prized in Mexico, and distant kinship relations are kept alive. Family ties are also extended through forms of ritual kinship such as the famous Mexican institution of *compadrazgo* (co-parenthood), which establishes a relationship between men and women as *compadres* and *comadres,* and cuts across social and class divisions.

As members of a society with a strong sense of local community, of family and of religion, Mexicans have a clear sense of identity and of place. Of course, there are factors operating in the opposite direction, too. The economy seems to have a disastrous crisis every decade; divorce rates, though still low, are increasing; and Mexico is becoming a more mobile society (more families are moving out of their local communities). It is difficult to tell how all of this will affect Mexican society at large, but with such a strong, exuberant national culture and heritage, how the society responds will be uniquely Mexican.

The Mexican Economy

Thirty percent of the population is engaged in agriculture, producing exports of coffee, cotton, fruit and vegetables, but the country has to import the staple food, maize (corn), to meet its needs. Industry, such as manufacturing steel, cars, chemicals, textiles and clothing, and assembling electronic parts for US manufacturers, occupies more than half the workforce. Mexico is the world's fourth-largest oil producer, with reserves of some 67 billion barrels. It leads the world in silver mining and is a leader in mining other minerals as well. Tourism attracts more than 19 million visitors a year, bringing Mexico an annual income of almost US$11 billion.

A BRIEF HISTORY

The history of Mexico is more a story of revolution than evolution. A sweeping view of history from the earliest civilisations up to the present finds a pattern that keeps repeating itself in the region: a civilisation flourishes, weakens and collapses, or is put to the sword by invaders. As the nation enters the third millennium, this pattern seems to be changing – and for the better.

Pre-Columbian Cultures

Before any civilisation inhabited this land, there were nomadic bands that subsisted by hunting and gathering. The prevailing theory on how they got here is that their ancestors crossed what is now the Bering Strait over a land bridge from Siberia to Alaska between 15,000 and 20,000 years ago. From Alaska, they moved southwards, arriving in what is now Mexico at least 10,000 years ago.

By around 4,000BC these hunter-gatherers discovered how to domesticate plants, among them maize. In the ensuing centuries, agricultural techniques were refined and extended to other crops, which in turn allowed for the settlement of large communities. By around 1200BC a remarkable civilisation emerged in the fertile lowlands along the Gulf Coast in what are now the Mexican states of Veracruz and Tabasco. We call these

A huge Olmec head, now in the Xalapa Archaeological Museum

The ancient 'ball game' re-enacted by a descendant of the Maya

people the Olmec, and their civilisation was a mother culture for all the peoples that came afterwards.

We have gleaned what we know of the Olmec from their ruined cities, their hieroglyphic writing system, and their distinctive, highly stylised art. This includes the famous stone heads that weigh many tons and portray human features, which on some heads look baby-faced and on others feline. They also left beautiful objects carved in jade. The Olmec established the cultural traits that would become universal among the many civilisations to come afterwards. They established a writing system, a simple calendar, a ritual ceremony that we call simply the 'ball game', and the construction of large ceremonial centres.

In their demise, the Olmec also set the pattern for later civilisations to follow – a cataclysmic decline. But before disappearing they greatly influenced the younger civilisations that sprang up in distant parts of Mexico and Central

America: the builders of the metropolis of Teotihuacán in the central highlands of Mexico, a people for whom history has no name; the Zapotecs of the southern highlands, who built the beautiful ceremonial complex at Monte Albán; and the Maya, who established several city-states in the lowlands of southeast Mexico, Guatemala and Honduras, including Palenque, Calakmul and Tikal.

The rise of these later civilisations define the Classic period of pre-Columbian civilisation in Mexico (AD300 to 900). The achievements of the Mayan civilisation in particular were spectacular: astronomers refined the calendar to an astonishing level of accuracy, mathematicians invented the 'zero', and scribes developed the epigraphic writing system that incorporated phonetics and prefixes and suffixes to indicate elaborate verb tenses.

This was a cosmopolitan age that saw great cultural and material exchange between distant city-states. The artistic achievement of the Classic period includes the grandest architecture of the pre-Columbian era, as a visit to Teotihuacán, Palenque or Monte Albán impressively confirms.

A traditional Maya home, made from wood and thatch

Later cities would be built on as grand a scale, but they wouldn't show the refinement in aesthetic expression – also found in sculptures, frescoes and ceramics – of this earlier age.

The city of Teotihuacán held the pre-eminent position. Evidence suggests that the city had various wards that were occupied by people from several distant lands and of different ethnic groups. At its zenith, Teotihuacán was probably the largest city in the world. It is here that the cult of the feathered serpent, later known as Quetzalcóatl, came to prominence.

Then it all came to an abrupt end. Teotihuacán was abandoned. There are signs of violence, but we do not know who inflicted it. The Zapotec culture that built Monte Albán likewise weakened and withdrew in the face of aggression from the neighbouring Mixtec. The classic Maya cities were also abandoned, and new Maya cities rose in their stead in the Yucatán to the north. At the close of the Classic period a people known as the Toltec began to flourish and filled the vacuum left by the abandonment of Teotihuacán. Their capital was at Tollán (Tula) in the present state of Hidalgo north of the valley of Mexico. They rose to prominence in the 10th century and had collapsed by the end of the 12th century.

The Plumed Serpent

In the Toltec pantheon, Quetzalcóatl, the plumed serpent, god of the morning star, the wind and arts, and his rival, Tezcatlipoca (lord of the smoking mirror, who represented sorcery and the night), were all-important. Early in the history of Tollán, there seems to have been some civil strife. The king Ce Acatl Topiltzín, a priest of Quetzalcóatl, was ousted by his bellicose brother, a supporter of Tezcatlipoca.

Topiltzín was pale-skinned and bearded – unusual characteristics among the Indians. Ousted from Tollán, he led his followers east, to the land of the Maya, who named him Kukulcán. Somewhere along the way, he acquired divine status, and was identified with the divine Quetzalcóatl. Legend has it that Topiltzín-Quetzalcóatl-Kukulcán sailed off to the east on a raft of snakes, but not before promising to return. That is why, four centuries later, when the Aztecs learned that pale-skinned bearded men had disembarked from 'floating houses', some may have concluded that the demigod had kept his promise.

The Toltec put greater emphasis on warfare and human sacrifice than earlier societies had and were more militaristic. But they were great traders as well, following many of the same routes established by the traders of Teotihuacán to distant parts of Mexico. There is obvious Toltec influence in the Post-classic Maya cities of the upper Yucatán, especially Chichén Itzá, which has a number of buildings that are startlingly similar to Tollán and a clear departure from Mayan architecture.

Daily life in Tenochtitlán, as seen by the muralist Diego Rivera

A century after the decline of the Toltec, a people known as the Aztec, or the Mexica, came to the central valley of Mexico. For them, warfare held an even more glorified position than it had for the Toltecs. The valley of Mexico at that time held the greatest concentration of people in Mexico (as it still does), distributed among several city-states that ringed three large lakes. At first, the Aztec survived as mercenaries for different city-states, eventually adopting much of the culture and refinement of these societies. They established their capital, Tenochtitlán, in the middle of a lake and, within less than a century, through shrewd alliances and well-planned military campaigns, made themselves masters of the entire valley. By the time the Spaniards arrived, Tenochtitlán was an impressive metropolis linked to the shore by great elevated causeways and criss-crossed by canals, in which there was a great traffic of boats.

The Aztec empire kept expanding, waging ever more distant wars across the central highlands, down to the lowlands in the east and into the southern mountain areas and beyond. Warfare was almost a continuous occupation. In time, war became a ritualised affair made necessary by the need to take prisoners who would satisfy the Aztec gods' need for human sacrifice. By the time the conquistadors arrived, the empire was racked by crisis: population pressures in the valley were high, relations between Tenochtitlán and its partner cities were tense, the Aztec ruling class was divided and military expansion had slowed.

The Conquest and the Colonial Era

When 600 Spaniards arrived at the gulf coast of central Mexico in 1519, they had, from their talks with coastal Indians, a general idea of the scope of the Aztec Empire that awaited them inland. Hernán Cortés, the Spanish leader, was a shrewd campaigner with an instinctual understanding of the hearts of men. In the conquest of this land, he eventually used this talent to manipulate every party who played a role: the soldiers under him; his superior, the Governor of Cuba; the Spanish military force that was later sent against him; the Indian rulers of the cities that paid tribute to the Aztec; Moctezuma, the Aztec ruler; and even the Spanish King Carlos V. With him was Doña Marina, an Indian slave who was presented to Cortés

Shrewd leader: Hernán Cortés

A depiction of the first encounter between Cortés and Moctezuma

as a gift, and who became his interpreter, his confidant and his mistress. She is known in Mexico today as La Malinche, a betrayer of her people (today in Mexico anyone acting unpatriotically may be called *malinchista*), but this is unfair because she was given to Cortés against her will.

One of the first things that Cortés did was burn his ships to prevent his men from considering retreat. Next, he entered into negotiations with Moctezuma, who sent envoys with gifts to persuade Cortés not to come to Tenochtitlán. Moctezuma was an indecisive and superstitious man. Unlike rulers before him, he had been a priest and was more in awe of omens and prophecies than his warriors. He was fully aware of the prediction of Quetzalcóatl's return and wished to keep the white men at a distance until he could decide what to do. His gifts only whetted the Spaniards' appetite for treasure. Cortés exploited Moctezuma's indecision, alternately cajoling and bullying his way to the Aztec capital, while stopping to make allies of the Aztecs' enemies.

The Spaniards arrived in Tenochtitlán in November of 1519, and were greeted with much pomp and ceremony. Cortés soon afterwards made a hostage of the Aztec ruler, hoping somehow to wrest control of the empire from him. Then came news of the landing of a second Spanish force with orders to take Cortés prisoner for disobeying his superior. Cortés quickly led a portion of his forces to meet the challenger and persuade him to join his endeavour. While he was gone a bloody incident occurred, forcing the Spaniards to flee the Aztec city with tremendous losses. Moctezuma was killed, either stoned by his own people or killed by the Spanish.

Cortés regrouped the Spanish forces and, with the help of their Indian allies, began slowly to gain military control over the highlands until he isolated Tenochtitlán and could lay siege to it. With the fall of the city, Aztec power crumbled and the colonialisation of New Spain (as it was called) began. The Spanish victory marked the end of Mexico's 3,000-year-old cultural tradition dating back to the Olmec. Temples were torn down and the stone used to build churches and Spanish palaces. Native books were burned and golden ornaments were melted into ingots and sent to Madrid.

The king rewarded Cortés for his actions with wealth, land grants and a title of nobility, while at the same time shifting control of the colony to a governing council. For the next three centuries, Spain would govern Mexico as a colony. It built the colonial capital on the ruins of Tenochtitlán, sent out expeditions in all directions to look for more wealth and to extend the borders of the colony, and issued to its Spanish subjects land grants, known as *encomiendas,* which also

Spanish rule as seen by the Jesuit missionary Ignacio Tirsch

provided a complement of Indian serfs. Soon after the conquest, gold and great quantities of silver ore were found in the mountains north and west of Mexico City, and the Spanish quickly founded several mining towns that were to become beautiful colonial cities.

The church became involved in the colony from the beginning. It faced the enormous task of bringing the teachings of the Christianity to millions of 'heathen' natives. Large numbers of evangelising priests crossed to the New World to be part of this mission. What they found horrified many, including Bishop Bartolomé de las Casas, who fought for the protection and rights of the Indians. Missions established by the church protected the Indians and their lands from encroachment by Spaniards. Many clerics learned the language and customs of their new wards and wrote valuable works describing what they found. With Indian labour, the Church erected churches, hospitals and convents that are some of the most beautiful buildings in the country. For the most part, the Indians embraced the new religion with fervour, and the great majority remain Roman Catholic to this day.

Monastery of San Antonio de Padua at Izamal (Yucatán)

The Spaniards brought with them cattle, sheep, pigs, chickens and horses (only the turkey and dog were native to Mexico – even mice came from Europe), sugar cane, bananas and oranges. Mexico in return gave Europe tomatoes, maize, vanilla, avocados, chocolate and peanuts. The Spaniards also imported diseases for which the native population had no natural defences: smallpox,

A Jesuit priest brings the Christian gospel to a group of Indians

chicken pox and different varieties of measles, as well as malaria from Africa brought in with slaves. The native population suffered a cataclysmic decline that reached its lowest level in the mid-17th century. In contrast, the *mestizo* population (the offspring of the union of European and Indian races) grew steadily throughout the colonial era. Above them in the hierarchy of colonial society were the *criollos* (people of European descent born in the New World) and at the top of the ladder were *peninsulares* (Spaniards born in Europe), who had the trust of the Spanish crown.

The Struggle for Independence

Friction between the *criollos* and the *peninsulares* grew steadily as the *criollos* found themselves excluded from power. Then in 1810 a *criollo* village priest, Father Miguel Hidalgo, gave the famous 'grito', the cry for independence, in the small town of Dolores, near present-day San Miguel de Allende. From Dolores, with his rag-tag peasant army, Hidalgo marched to Guanajuato, where he laid siege to the town's granary-turned-fortress, the Alhóndiga, and won his first victory. To this day, the Alhóndiga shows the scars from that battle. Its formidable walls must have proved daunting to any besieging force lacking artillery. The movement soon became a full-fledged revolt that was put down by the government only after great difficulty and the execution of Hidalgo and his lieutenants.

But from this effort sprang others, notably the military campaigns waged by the *mestizo* priest José María Morelos in southern and western Mexico. This was a more convincing and more radical attack on colonial society than Father Hidalgo's struggle, and it horrified the conservative colonial élite, who dedicated enormous resources towards isolating Morelos's forces and cutting off his supply lines. Morelos was

Father Miguel Hidalgo spearheads the struggle for independence

finally defeated and executed in 1815, but not before he had introduced the issues of democratic election and the redistribution of land into the political discourse of the day. In an ironic twist, a liberal government came to power in Spain in 1820 and drove the conservative royalists to join the ranks of those fighting for independence.

It was left to the *criollo* leader of the royalist forces, Agustín de Iturbide, to effect independence in a smooth manner, which he did by uniting his forces with those of the independence movement. The Spanish viceroy was left with no alternative but to abandon his office and return to Spain. After a brief period under the dictatorship of Iturbide, Mexico attempted a republican form of government but with little success. Political struggles between the different parties – centralist and federalist, conservative and liberal –

> **In the first 30 years of independence, Mexico had 50 governments, mostly the result of military coups, and 11 of them presided over by General Antonio López de Santa Anna, who earned himself the title of 'perpetual dictator'.**

prevented any stable government. Endless internal struggles, in addition to poor leadership and the consequences of the long fight for independence, sapped Mexico's energy and made the country vulnerable to foreign incursions. An extortionist expedition by the French blockaded Veracruz in 1838, and Mexico lost half its territory in a disastrous war with the United States in 1848.

Throughout the 1850s the struggle for control of the Mexican government pitted the conservatives, who favoured the large landholders and the church, against the liberals, who held to the ideas of 19th-century liberalism and represented the *mestizo* majority and small businessmen. They advocated an end to the privileges tenjoyed by the church and the *hacendados* (owners of haciendas or large landholdings). In the Constitution of 1857, the Liberals managed to get several anticlerical measures passed into law that required the church to sell off its vast landholdings. As a result, rich Mexicans and foreign speculators gained possession of lands that the church had traditionally allowed Indian communities to cultivate.

In the last part of the decade, a civil war broke out which ended in victory for the liberals. Benito Juárez, one of the most fascinating figures of Mexican history, became president. Juárez, a Zapotec Indian orphaned at three, did not speak Spanish until the age of 12. Educated for the priesthood in Oaxaca, he turned to law and in time became governor of Oaxaca state and drafter of the anticlerical provisions of the 1857 Constitution. Juárez inherited a difficult situation. With the National Treasury empty, he had to suspend payment on the debts that Mexico owed to foreign powers including Spain, Britain and France. Emperor Napoleon III, seeking to extend French influence in the Americas, used this failure to meet payments as a cause for invading Mexico.

Maximilian of Habsburg, briefly Emperor of Mexico

His first attempt was not a success. On 5 May 1862 (celebrated as *cinco de mayo*), a poorly equipped and small Mexican army managed to defeat a superior and well-armed French invasion force at Puebla. The French, however, were back the next year with an even larger force and took control of Mexico City, installing a supporter of France's goals in Mexico, Maximilian of Habsburg, as Emperor. Juárez set up an

Maximilian of Habsburg, a liberal and an idealist, enacted reforms to the working conditions and wages of adults and children, making corporal punishment illegal. He also introduced the collective ownership of land and cancelled all debts over 10 pesos.

alternative government in the provinces, doing what he could to wage a guerrilla war against the occupying forces until the French, exhausted by the effort of trying to keep order in Mexico, withdrew their forces and abandoned Maximilian to his fate. He was executed in Querétaro in 1867.

Juárez was reinstalled as president and immediately set to work restoring the economy and improving conditions in the countryside. By then, Mexico had lived through more than 50 years of constant political strife, been occupied twice by foreign invasion forces, and had suffered several civil wars. In five years, Juárez managed to establish order, stability and economic development within the country. He died of natural causes in 1872. Four years later, General Porfirio Díaz came to power in a coup d'état. He held office for the next 34 years, a period known in Mexico as the Porfiriato.

During this time, economic development boomed, especially mining and oil drilling and the construction of railways. Foreign investment increased; showy public construction projects such as theatres and opera houses were carried out in cities across the country. But these advances did little to benefit the poor, who were exploited in the most inhumane manner in some regions. Harsh social conditions prevailed in rural areas, where the poor were forced off the land they had worked for themselves and were made into wage labourers for haciendas. The *hacendados* paid very little and would ensure the workers couldn't leave by providing food, drink and clothing on credit to bind them to the hacienda through debt peonage. These conditions created a large mass of people with little to lose and a lot to avenge.

It was dissatisfaction with Díaz among the middle and the provincial upper classes that eventually put an end to the Porfiriato. Mexicans of the landed classes resented the sweet government deals given to the railways and other foreign-owned companies. They also resented Díaz's stranglehold on power, which he held as a dictator, with the formality of rigged elections every four years.

The Revolution and Modern Times

In response to the call of Francisco I. Madero, the exiled former governor of Coahuila who had been Díaz's main opposition in the last election, armed revolts broke out in several parts of the country on 20 November 1910. Pancho Villa in the northern state of Chihuahua and Emiliano Zapata in the southern state of Morelos were the most famous of the revolutionary commanders. So ill-prepared were Díaz's forces for a broad-based insurrection that within six months the dictator was on a boat headed for exile and Madero was installed as the new president of Mexico.

For Madero, the aim of the Revolution was to provide constitutional reforms such as one-term offices for presidents, but for most of those in the ranks of the revolutionary forces, the causes were workers' rights, an end to debt peonage, land reform and other social issues. But before conflict on these issues could crystallise, Madero was betrayed and murdered by his chief of staff, Victoriano Huerta, who assumed control of the government. The revolutionary forces under Zapata and Villa, along with Alvaro Obregón and

Hacienda Yaxcopoil near Mérida, preserved as a museum

Venustiano Carranza, the governor of Coahuila, returned to the battlefield. In a series of violent, hard-fought victories, Villa and the other commanders destroyed the federal forces and drove Huerta into exile. In these and subsequent conflicts, acts of cruelty were committed on both sides, and human life was held cheap. It is estimated that two million Mexicans died in the Mexican Revolution.

Now it was Carranza's turn to become president. He came from the same educated, land-owning class of northern Mexico as Madero and was just as conservative on social issues, especially land reform. A constitutional assembly was convened to thrash out the differences between the different sides. It failed, and conflict arose between Villa, Zapata and Carranza. Zapata remained true to the idea of land reform and did not see Carranza as a friend of the people. Villa, thanks to his great popularity, was a threat to Carranza's power. Hostilities broke out, and after some initial victories, Villa was defeated by Obregón and banished to Chihuahua. Zapata, staying close to his power base in Morelos, could not be beaten, so Carranza found a way to lure him out into the open and murder him. This cost Carranza his political support and made it impossible for him to keep the presidency. He was murdered in rural Veracruz while trying to flee the country.

Obregón succeeded Carranza. He gave social reform plenty of lip service but did little more than make token gestures. During his presidency, Pancho Villa was assassinated in Chihuahua. Obregón was succeeded by Plutarco Elías Calles, a shrewd man who may have been involved in Obregón's subsequent assassination (when Obregón broke one of the tenets of the Revolution by running for president a second time).

Revolutionary hero Pancho Villa

This left Calles as the government's strong-man. He established the foundations for the government party that became the Partido Revolucionario Institucional (Instituted Revolutionary Party, or PRI). He also established the system of one-party rule and proceeded to govern Mexico through a succession of puppet presidents until Lázaro Cárdenas forced him into exile in 1936. Once this was done, Cárdenas began fulfilling many of the promises of the Revolution, especially land reform and the nationalisation of the foreign-owned oil industry. He became a wildly popular figure and remains so to this day in many parts of the country.

Cárdenas stepped down at the end of his term in 1940 and retired from party politics. This set a pattern through which the PRI maintained political stability and the smooth transition of

> **Cárdenas created *ejidos*, peasant cooperatives, to which he redistributed 18 million hectares (45 million acres) of land. In less than six years, his government granted land to one-third of the population.**

power through an orderly succession of presidents. Each president enjoyed one six-year term in which he dictated the actions of the national government with few constraints. In the fifth year, he personally chose his successor, who would begin a vigorous national political campaign with all the trappings of a democratic electoral contest (though until recently the outcome of the election was never in doubt). In the sixth year, the president retired from government – in many cases with a large personal fortune, the source of which was never quite revealed.

By the end of the 20th century, the one-party system was being strained by changes in Mexican society, especially the strengthening of the middle class and the growing independence of a large national business sector. The urban poor and the peasants demonstrated political muscle: there was a show of strength by a peasant army in Chiapas known as the Zapatistas and large demonstrations by several organisations of the poor in the capital. In addition, a series of economic crises and political scandals weakened the PRI enough to provide an opening for two credible opposition parties – the conservative Partido Acción Nacional (PAN), which has its base in the relatively rich northern half of the country, and the leftist PRD, led by Lázaro Cárdenas's son, Cuauhtémoc. These parties stripped the PRI of its legislative majority and gained control of several state governments. The PRI responded by making itself more democratic. Under President Ernesto Zedillo the party held political primaries in several states to allow the rank and file, not the bosses, to choose the party's candidates.

For the presidential election in 2000, Zedillo refused to name a candidate and instead established a procedure for holding primary elections across the country. For the first time in more than seven decades, the PRI lost the presidential election to the PAN.

Many believe that the new president, Vicente Fox, can find solutions to many of the country's social and economic problems. While he is still in office and it is still too early to fully understand his impact on the country, observers have noted that many in Mexico are showing a greater interest in politics and are carrying out the discussions and making the demands that are necessary to a growing democracy. For his part, Fox has encouraged this debate, introducing a freedom of information act that made public millions of secret government intelligence files.

So far, it appears as if Mexico may, for the first time in its history, use political evolution rather than revolution to bring about a new system of government.

An eagle perched on a cactus is now the national symbol of Mexico

Historical Highlights

1000–300BC The flourishing of the Olmec, the first civilisation and the mother culture of pre-Columbian Mexico.

AD 300–800 The age of the classic pre-Columbian civilisations of Mexico (Teotihuacán, the Maya and the Zapotec); a period of great artistic and intellectual evolution.

900–1230 The Toltec establish their capital at Tollán and control most of central Mexico. Their influence extends all the way to the Yucatán, especially in the Mayan city of Chichén Itzá.

1350–1519 The Aztec control all of central and southern Mexico from their highland capital of Tenochtitlán.

1521 Hernán Cortés conquers Mexico for the Spanish crown.

1521–1821 Spain rules the colony through a succession of viceroys. The church actively converts the Indians to Christianity. Silver is discovered in great quantities, making Spain the richest country in Europe.

1810 The priest Miguel Hidalgo initiates the struggle for independence from Spain.

1821 Agustín de Iturbide gains independence for Mexico and soon afterwards makes himself emperor.

1823–1861 A period of political turmoil and civil wars.

1848 Mexico is defeated in a war with the US and surrenders more than half its territory.

1862–1864 The French invade Mexico and establish Maximilian as Emperor. French defeated by Mexican Nationalist forces under Benito Juárez.

1876–1910 Rule of dictator Porfirio Díaz, who encourages foreign investments, especially in the construction of railways.

1910–1929 The Mexican Revolution, which calls for reforms in the name of social equality, and single-term presidencies.

1938 Lázaro Cárdenas expropriates American and British oil companies and nationalises railways and all mineral resources.

1985 Massive earthquake causes thousands of deaths in Mexico City.

1988–1999 Political, electoral reforms weaken the PRI's one-party rule.

2000 Vicente Fox becomes first non-PRI president in 71 years.

WHERE TO GO

We use Mexico City as our starting point, then describe side trips and regional itineraries. Wherever your travels in Mexico take you, even a brief visit to Mexico City is in order. Getting to know the thriving capital is the only way truly to understand this captivating country – veiled in mysticism, infused with an appreciation of the present moment and proud of its colourful heritage.

MEXICO CITY

With a history extending over 2,000 years, Mexico City has served as a centre of culture and commerce for ancient civilisations, European conquistadors and modern Latin America. The capital is centre stage for all aspects of national life – political, financial, intellectual and social. It is a magnet that has drawn nearly one out of five Mexicans to its 350 sprawling *colonias,* the elegant suburbs, crowded neighbourhoods and ramshackle squatter settlements that hold an estimated 23 million souls. Big as it is, Mexico City is not a metropolis that overpowers, although recent economic hardships have led to a significant increase in crime. It is a remarkable city to visit and, with a wealth of historical and cultural attractions, well worth exploring. Most of its attractions for the tourist lie along the 5-km (3-mile) long axis between the Bosque de Chapultepec park and the Zócalo.

The Zócalo

The official name of this central square is the **Plaza de la Constitución**, but most residents refer to it as *zócalo,* or pedestal, which was all that remained when an equestrian

A Maya *chac-mool* in the Temple of the Warriors in Chichén Itzá

statue of Spain's King Carlos IV was removed after independence. Now, central plazas all over Mexico are informally called 'the zócalo'.

The vast, unadorned square (240m/790ft on each side) covers the very centre of what used to be Tenochtitlán, the city the Aztecs founded in 1325. With its solitary flagpole bearing a massive Mexican flag, the constant buzz of activity and the grandeur of its surrounding buildings – which include the remains of an Aztec pyramid, an ornate colonial cathedral, the stoic centre of national government and towering, modern structures in the background – the zócalo imparts a sense of the layers of history and culture that combine to make modern Mexico.

The zócalo stands on the site of an Aztec market that was once bordered by brightly painted pyramids and palaces. This is how Bernal Díaz del Castillo, one of Cortés' soldiers,

The cathedral displays a heady mixture of architectural styles

described it: 'We were astounded at the great number of people and the quantities of merchandise… dealers in gold, silver and precious stones, feathers, cloaks and embroidered goods and male and female slaves… choco-

> Mexico City is served by a metro system with nine lines and 125 stations. Some attractive stations also function as centres for shopping and socialising.

late merchants… those who sold sisal cloth and ropes and the sandals they wear on their feet… Then there were the fruit sellers and the women who sold cooked food, flour and honey cake and tripe… pottery of all kinds… timber, boards, cradles, beams, paper and some reeds that smell of liquid amber and are full of tobacco… Some of our soldiers who had been in many parts of the world, in Constantinople, in Rome and all over Italy, said that they had never seen a market so well laid out, so large, so orderly and so full of people.'

Much as the conquistadores admired the market and the rest of Tenochtitlán, they demolished the city, filling in the canals to make streets and using the Aztec stone to build the metropolis that has grown into present-day Mexico City. They called the open centre the Plaza de Armas, a military parade ground.

The **Catedral Metropolitana** (Metropolitan Cathedral, open Tues–Sun 10.30am–2.30pm), on the north end of the square, was begun in 1573, and by the time the towers were completed in 1813 it incorporated the styles of many architects and artists, inside and out. The north and west sides reflect the austerity of 16th-century Castille; Baroque and Neoclassical elements appear in the main, southern façade; Rococo breaks loose in some of the interior chapels, notably in the Altar de los Reyes, the 'Altar of the Kings', an intricate concoction of carved wood covered with gold leaf, harbouring many a hand-wringing saint with eyes cast heavenward and paintings darkened by age and smoke. The cathedral is big, as befits its site and role, and incorporates 51 domes, including the central cupola designed by Manuel Tolsá.

Many of the 14 chapels were damaged in a 1967 fire, but have been restored. The second on the right holds the black Cristo del Veneno (Christ of the Poison). Legend has it that a local bishop who had been poisoned was saved when he kissed the image, which drew out the venom, shrivelled up and turned black. The last chapel on the left is dedicated to San Felipe de Jesús, the first Mexican-born saint, who was martyred in 1597 while attempting to convert the Japanese. It also contains the ashes of Augustín de Iturbide, a royalist commander during the struggle for independence who declared Mexico an independent country and himself its emperor, and the throne upon which he was crowned.

Market outside the Sagrario

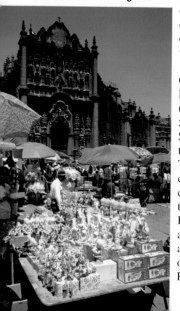

Tilting away from the Cathedral on the right is **El Sagrario Metropolitano** (Sanctuary, open daily 11am–5pm), dedicated in 1768 to Santiago (St James), the patron saint of Mexico City. The two façades and finely carved doors of this smaller church are considered masterpieces of the extravagant Baroque style that Spanish architect José Churriguera adopted and adapted throughout 18th-century Mexico. Its Renaissance elements, such as inverted obelisks, Greek columns and pilasters, and garlands and cornices are tumultuously assembled and leave no space empty. The two churches, like a number of other buildings in the central district, have been sinking and sagging for years and are now supported on pilings. Draining the surrounding lake and pumping water have caused the slow

The Templo Mayor excavation

subsidence of the land on which they 'floated'. A major restoration effort that included reinforcing the subsoil has saved the buildings from probable collapse.

Beside the Sagrario, a model of Tenochtitlán sits in a basin of water that represents Lake Texcoco. The three causeways linking the island city with the land intersected at what was the ceremonial centre of Moctezuma's empire. The sacred enclosure was 150m (500ft) square and held 78 buildings, including the Royal Palace.

Just beyond the Sagrario a wall encloses the excavations of the **Templo Mayor**, the pyramid to the Aztec gods of rain and war, Tláloc and Huitzilopochtli (open Tues–Sun 9am–5pm). Colonial buildings covered the site until 1978, when work on a new metro uncovered a beautifully carved stone disc 3m (10ft) in diameter depicting the moon goddess Coyolxauhqui with her head and limbs severed. According to legend, her brother Huitzilopochtli, the sun god, threw her from the top of a hill as punishment for rebellion. The find pinpointed the site of his great temple, for the disk of the dismembered goddess was placed at its base to represent the struggle between the sun and the moon.

The ancient Mexicans always enlarged these monuments by building on top of the previous structure, removing nothing. Archaeologists have uncovered seven layers of the Templo Mayor and a treasure trove of offerings to the gods underneath. These are displayed in the handsome **Museo del Templo Mayor** (open Tues–Sun 9am–5pm). The museum overlooks the site and is divided into sections representing the two temples. The entrance fee includes access to the excavations. The museum's bookshop has one of the best selections of foreign-language titles on Mexican art and antiquity.

The **Palacio Nacional** (open Mon–Sat 10am–6pm) takes up the east side of the zócalo. This is the seat of government, as indeed it was when the palace of Moctezuma occupied the site. The Aztec emperor kept a collection of animals, water birds and fish here in what was the first zoo in the Americas. Cortés claimed the entire property and his son Martín sold it to

The courtyard of the Palacio Nacional

Spain. The present structure, begun in 1693 (the Spanish Viceroys lived in an earlier building), has served as a prison, army barracks and home of the first Mexican Congress. It was enlarged by Maximilian, the emperor sent by France to govern Mexico during the 1860s, and a third storey was added in 1927. The President's office is in an inner courtyard, though he frequently works in his residence, 'Los Pinos', in Bosque de Chapultepec.

> Diego Rivera, a friend of Trotsky and a lifelong Marxist, combined his revolutionary convictions and nationalist ideals in a style that incorporated indigenous Mexican imagery. His bold large-scale murals stimulated a revival of fresco painting in Latin America.

At 11pm on 15 September, the zócalo fills with people when the President reads Father Hidalgo's declaration of independence, the 'Grito de Dolores', from the central balcony. Hanging above him is the liberty bell from Hidalgo's church, which rings on Mexico's national holiday, answered by the great 12-ton bell of the cathedral. The central portal of the Palacio Nacional leads to a patio where a broad staircase ascends beneath Diego Rivera's murals of the history of Mexico. It's all here, with the whole cast of thousands spread out along three walls.

The account begins on the right, before the Conquest, with the god Quetzalcóatl sailing across the sky and an upside-down sun god bringing food and life to the world. In the centre, the Spaniards battle with the Aztec eagle and jaguar knights. The Church burns Mayan books, the Inquisition strangles heretics, Father Hidalgo rallies the population for Independence, American soldiers invade Veracruz, and Zapata proclaims 'Tierra y Libertad'. On the left, Karl Marx points to the future, while Diego Rivera's wife, the artist Frida Kahlo, represents education as the hope of the people. Other

Rivera panels depicting different indigenous tribes encircle the second floor arcade.

Between the Palacio Nacional and the Suprema Corte (Supreme Court) building to the south is the **Acequia Real**, once a canal, then a street and now a likeness of the canal, with grass replacing water. The zócalo's south side is occupied by the Departamento del Distrito Federal (Federal District building) and the old City Hall. To the east, the garden, restaurant and bar on the roof of the Hotel Majestic offer a terrific view of the whole plaza. Two blocks north is the **Nacional Monte de Piedad** (National Pawn Shop), its rooms filled with an amazing collection of unclaimed items for sale. You just might find an attractive antique ring here amid the busts of Beethoven, old radios and musty sofas.

The Centro Histórico

The zócalo is the heart of the *centro histórico*, old Mexico City. Its streets are studded with colonial palaces and churches, enchanting squares and many museums. The area behind the cathedral is a diverse marketplace, with each street known for its particular speciality, be it books, wedding dresses or sewing machines. For example, hundreds of concoctions from medicinal plants are sold in an alley off Calle República de Guatemala. República de Brasil leads into the Plaza de Santo Domingo, one of the capital's most picturesque corners. Under the arcades, public scribes type documents, fill in complicated government forms, or even compose love letters for illiterate or tongue-tied clients.

Stop by the 18th-century **Templo de Santo Domingo** to see the chapel on the right with a wall covered with *milagros*, small silver arms, legs, eyes and other bits of anatomy offered in thanks for recovery from illness. You'll see these *milagros* (also known as *ex-votos*) and *retablos* (primitive paintings on tin) in churches all over the country.

Take Calle Obregón from the square and turn left on Calle Argentina to the **Secretaría de Educación Pública** (Ministry of Public Education, open Mon–Fri 10am–5pm). More than a hundred of Diego Rivera's earliest (1923) and best murals cover the walls of the courtyard, staircases and upper floors of the ministry. Look for the lively *Day of the Dead* scene in the left rear of the patio.

While Rivera was at work here, his contemporaries David Alfaro Siqueiros and José Clemente Orozco were painting frescos in the **Colegio de San Idelfonso** around the corner (to compare the

A public scribe plies his trade on the Plaza de Santo Domingo

work of these three Mexican masters, follow Calle Argentina a block towards the zócalo and turn left to 16 Calle Justo Sierra). Orozco's powerful and bitter scenes of injustice and war cover walls on three floors of the inner patio. On Calle de la Moneda, on the north flank of the Palacio Nacional, the first printing press in the western hemisphere was operating in 1536. After the street becomes Calle Zapata, it leads to Empress Carlota's favourite church, **La Santísima**, with a Churrigueresque façade rivalling the Sagrario's.

Three blocks south of the Palacio Nacional on Avenida Pino Suárez, the **Museo de la Ciudad de México** (Mexico City Museum, open Tues–Sun 10am–6pm) is housed in the

imposing colonial mansion of the Counts of Santiago Cali-
maya. Water spouts in the form of cannons overhang the
street. The museum provides a good overview of the city's
history from prehistoric to modern times, with maps, paintings, models, engravings and relics from every period.
Across the avenue an inscription marks the spot where
Moctezuma first met Cortés. Behind it is the **Hospital de
Jesús** (open Mon–Fri 9am–4pm, Sat 9am–1pm), founded by
Cortés and still functioning. The bust in the courtyard is one
of very few memorials to Cortés in Mexico, where he is regarded as a perpetrator of genocide.

The centro histórico is experiencing a renaissance in
nightlife. Despite the fact that the area essentially clears out
after dark, a number of hip clubs have opened in exquisite
Baroque and Art Deco buildings. Dancing to techno in such
a historic ambience is one of the ambiguous pleasures of
Mexico City.

Plaza Garibaldi, at the northern edge of the historic district on the Paseo de la Reforma, remains an important landmark as the gathering place for mariachis. However, the
square has earned a new notoriety – it is now known as one
of the highest crime areas in Mexico City, a meeting point
for young criminals who make their living by separating visitors from their personal belongings. Even so, Plaza Garibaldi is a must-see, perhaps as the first stop on your evening
rounds (while the ambience might not be as lively as it is
after midnight, the plaza is definitely a lot safer at this time).
Mariachis start drifting into the little plaza and will be there
until the early hours of the morning. Notice the statues of
well-loved popular musicians around the plaza.

The Alameda

For more traditional pleasures, retire to the leafy island of
the **Alameda Central**, about six blocks due south of Plaza

Garibaldi along the Reforma and next to the Palacio de Bellas Artes. Mexico City's first park was created in the late 16th century by draining a pond and planting the poplar trees (*álamos*), after which it is named. In the 18th and 19th centuries this was the centre of fashion, off-limits to the common people. Today it is a favourite place for a Sunday family outing amid romantic statuary and fountains. Huge clusters of fancifully designed balloons bob along in the clutch of vendors, while children clamour for ice cream and lovers embrace on the benches. This is where heretics were burned at the stake during the Inquisition. There are musical performances in the Moorish bandstand at weekends.

The scene is amusingly captured in Rivera's mural *A Dream of a Sunday Afternoon in the Alameda Park*, created for the old Del Prado Hotel on Avenida Juárez, which skirts the southern flank of the plaza. The hotel was wrecked by the 1985 earthquake, but the mural was spared and now has its home in the **Museo Mural Diego Rivera** (open Tues– Sun 10am–6pm) at the western end of the park. The display documents the fracas that erupted when the mural was unveiled and found to have the words *Dios no existe* ('There is no God') on a paper held by one of

Fountain in the Alameda

Rivera's subjects. After much controversy, the offending sentence was removed. Rivera himself appears as a pudgy boy holding the hand of a lady skeleton wrapped in a feathered serpent boa. Next door is the **Pinacoteca Virreinal**, exhibiting colonial period paintings in a former monastery.

At 89 Avenida Juárez, the **FONART** (National Foundation for the Support of Handicrafts) shop displays craftwork from all over Mexico (open Mon–Sat 10am–7pm). This is one of several FONART shops throughout the country. The large marble monument across the way is the Hemiciclo, dedicated to Benito Juárez. Tour guides joke that the **Torre Latinoamericano**, the city's first skyscraper, towering over

The Torre Latinoamericana

Avenida Juárez just east of the Alameda, is 'the highest skyscraper in the world' – the first of its 42 floors is 2,415m (7,925ft) above sea level. The observation deck is a good place to watch the sun go down (open daily 9.30am–11pm). Most of the building has been vacated and there are plans to turn it into a hotel. A monastery founded by the Franciscans in 1525 once stood here, but it was destroyed in the 19th-century Reform. The sunken **Iglesia de San Francisco** behind the tower is all that's left.

Across the Avenida Hidalgo, the broad avenue that forms the Alameda's northern border, is the **Iglesia de San Hipólito**, known for the statue of San Judas Tadeo, patron saint of lost causes. Also look for the tablet carved in 1599 of an eagle carrying an Indian in its claws. If you follow Avenida Hidalgo west across the Reforma, you'll come to the Hotel Cortés, which occupies a 17th-century building that once provided lodgings to visiting monks. Its attractive patio is a good spot to rest and enjoy a coffee or *cerveza* (beer). Hidalgo, inci-

Marble sculpture lines the façade of the Palacio de Bellas Artes

dentally, follows the path of the causeway on which the Spaniards fought their way out of Tenochtitlán on the Noche Triste, a night in which the Aztecs dealt a strong blow to the Spanish army, who fled for this one night before returning to conquer the capital.

On the northern side of the Alameda, between two facing churches sunk below the level of Hidalgo, the **Museo Franz Mayer** (open Mon–Sat 10am–5pm) is beautifully installed in the former San Juan de Dios hospital. Mayer, a German-born businessman, was a collector of all things Mexican: furniture, sculpture, church images, ceramics and curiosities such as an exquisite mosaic composed of bits of bright feathers. There is a cafeteria and a peaceful patio where you can relax listening to classical music. The church to the right, Santa Vera Cruz, is so steeply tipped that the aisle goes uphill.

The **Palacio de Bellas Artes** (Fine Arts Palace, open Tues–Sun 10am–6pm), at the eastern end of the Alameda, is

The Ballet Folklórico de México stages regional dance programmes in the Palacio de Bellas Artes, where the theatre has a famous curtain made by Tiffany from thousands of pieces of stained glass depicting Popocatépetl and Iztaccíhuatl. Light played on the curtain recreates dawn and sunset on the mountains.

a not-so-fine white marble Victorian pile typical of the grandiose projects of the dictator Porfirio Díaz. The interior, however, has a pure Art Deco rotunda and staircase of the 1920s leading to galleries where you can see murals all in one place by the Big Four of Mexican painting, Rivera, Siqueiros, Orozco and Tamayo.

The central post office is just across the Avenida Lázaro Cárdenas from the Bellas Artes and just beyond it, on Calle Tacuba, is the **Museo Nacional de Arte** (open Tues–Sun 10.30am–5.30pm). The art collection is heavy on 19th-century works, but there are interesting pieces from pre-Conquest times. The statue in front is El Caballito ('the Little Horse' – not little at all but an equestrian statue of Charles IV of Spain), originally erected in the zócalo in 1803, then moved to the university patio, then to the Paseo de la Reforma and finally, in 1981, to its present site. Coin collectors will enjoy the **Museo de la Numismática** (open Mon–Fri 10am–6pm) on the first floor of the Banco de México building adjoining the post office.

Three blocks south of the Museum, on Calle Madero, is the **Casa de los Azulejos** (House of Tiles), built in 1596 for the Count of Valle de Orizaba and covered in beautiful 18th-century blue-and-white tiles from Puebla. The Sanborns restaurant chain has converted the elegant inner court into a restaurant where homesick gringos flock to get a solid breakfast and hamburgers. You'll be served under a balcony where the suitor of the daughter of Valle de Orizaba was hanged after murdering the Count on the staircase. Down the street at number 17 is the **Palacio de Iturbide**, where General Agustín de Iturbide was proclaimed Emperor of Mexico in 1822. The palace now houses a bank, but frequent temporary exhibits are held on the beautiful patio (open daily 10am–7pm).

Two of the city's liveliest handicraft markets are a 10-minute walk south of the Alameda. The **Mercado de Artesanías de San Juan** (open Mon–Sat 9am–7pm, Sun 9am–4pm) is on Calle Ayuntamiento, just off Calle López, Mexico City's Chinatown. Scores of little

Decorative tiles on the Casa de los Azulejos

shops on two floors of this arcade sell the full range of Mexican crafts. The **Mercado de Artesanías de la Ciudadela** (open daily 10.30am–6.30pm) is five blocks down Calle Balderas on the Plaza de la Ciudadela. Here you can watch artisans weaving, painting and hammering away on their products. La Ciudadela on this square is a former arsenal, now the national library.

About 10 blocks east of La Ciudadela on Fray Servando T. de Mier, is one of Mexico's most bewitching markets, the **Mercado de Sonora** (daily 9am–6pm). It is an unusual market offering an opportunity to visit the world of magic and spells that surrounds the daily lives of residents of

Mexico City. Next to the stalls that sell plastic and ceramic pots and all the fixings for a successful wedding or birthday party, you can find all manner of magical potions, as well as alum to counteract negative forces, black salt and candles of every colour, for whatever ritual you might be interested in holding. There are experts in love potions and the ever-important *limpias* (cleansings) to dismiss any spell that may have been cast upon you by a jealous lover or an envious co-worker. Tarot card readings and even santería registers are offered here, conducted by real-life shamans. You will also find live black roosters, white hens and multicoloured birds, along with eggs of every colour and size. Hundreds of herbs that will cure every ailment are sold in the market, next to amulets and talismans to bring good luck to an enterprise, or guard your house from evil spirits.

An Indian stallholder sells maize at a city market

North and South along La Reforma

The **Paseo de la Reforma** is the principal avenue of Mexico City and one of the world's great boulevards. Conceived on a grand scale by Emperor Maximilian, it is still able to handle the monumental growth in traffic without losing its majestic ambience. The Reforma proper is the straight stretch between the Alameda and Chapultepec Park, though additions continue from both ends. Maximilian in-

Modern sculpture along Paseo de la Reforma

tended it to link his residence in Chapultepec castle with the seat of government in the Palacio Nacional on the zócalo (though the palace lies far east of the course the Reforma eventually took). This grand scheme was to be called the 'Avenue of Illustrious Men', lined with their statues. Porfirio Díaz completed the central section and unveiled the first of the statues, very few of whose subjects would qualify as illustrious today.

Agile windscreen-washing boys pounce on cars when they stop for the traffic lights on the Reforma. One intersection becomes a stage for jugglers and acrobats, another is the night-time turf of a kid who takes a mouthful of petrol from a can and blows out a plume of fire, then runs to collect pesos from drivers. Here and there you may spot one of the few remaining Victorian mansions that once lined the avenue. Now they are in the shadow of some of the hemisphere's most arresting modern office buildings. Look for the new

Bolsa, the Stock Exchange, an angular sandwich of two-tone glass layers beside a multifaceted beehive of mirrored panels.

Along the stretch of La Reforma north of the Alameda there are several places of interest, although this area of Mexico City is generally not known for tourist attractions. One popular site is Mexico's main flea market, the **Mercado de la Lagunilla** (Mon–Fri 10am–7pm, Sun 8am–6pm), found just east of the intersection of the Reforma, with Calle Lázaro Cárdenas at the roundabout marked by the statue of José Martí. Everything imaginable is sold here. This is the place to practise your bargaining and to spend an entertaining Sunday morning. Although the street market takes place only on Sundays, there are a few permanent stalls open the rest of the week as well.

The significance of the **Plaza de las Tres Culturas** is summed up in its name – the Square of Three Cultures – and is yet another visual monument to the depth and wealth of Mexican culture and history. It is near the northeastern end of the Reforma in what was the important Aztec market town of Tlatelolco. The ruins of a temple pyramid are overlooked by the colonial church of San Francisco and the modern glass and steel ministry of foreign affairs, hence the three cultures. The final battle of the conquest was fought here and a plaque movingly records the event: 'On 13 August 1521, heroically defended by Cuauhtémoc, Tlatelolco fell into the hands of Hernán Cortés. It was neither a triumph nor a defeat: it was the painful birth of the *mestizo* nation that is Mexico today.'

Another plaque here records yet another painful event that took place in the square. On 2 October 1968, only 10 days before the Olympic ceremonies began in Mexico City, the government killed hundreds of students who were peacefully protesting here. The plaque records the names of some of those murdered and is also dedicated to those whose names are still unknown.

Continuing along the northern extension of the Reforma known as Calzada de Guadalupe, 4km (2½ miles) beyond the Plaza de las Tres Culturas, you will come to one of the world's great religious shrines and the centre of Catholic Mexico, the **Basílica de la Virgen de Guadalupe**. Ten years after the Conquest, a newly baptised Indian named Juan Diego had a vision of the Virgin, who requested that a church be built in her honour on this site (an Aztec temple to the mother of the gods had once stood here but was razed by the Spaniards). The bishop was suspicious of Juan Diego's tale. The Virgin again appeared to the Indian, instructing him to pick roses and take them to the bishop as proof of the request. Roses miraculously appeared on the rocky hillside and Juan Diego collected them in his cloak. But when he took them to the doubting prelate, instead of roses, the cloak had Mary's image imprinted upon it. Convinced by this

The Apparition of the Virgin in the garden of the Basílica

miracle, the bishop ordered the church built to display the cloak. The image remains to this day, a mystery to scientists seeking to explain this modest cloth that is more than 450 years old. The present Basílica is the fifth to hold this relic – visitors can view the cloak close up from an underpass beside the altar without disturbing the mass.

The Virgin of Guadalupe is the true patron saint of Mexico and most of Latin America. Her feast is celebrated on 12 December: hundreds of thousands of believers from all over the world flock to the Basílica to pay homage, with many starting their pilgrimages months in advance to arrive in Mexico City on this sacred day. It is common to see people end their pilgrimage by walking on their knees the whole length of the Calzada de Guadalupe (close to 3km/2 miles) as a sign of their true devotion to the Virgin, or to thank her for some miracle she has granted. While there is a festive air surrounding the whole event, the occasion is a solemn one, and is one of Mexico's most impressive celebrations.

Geometric modern architecture along the Paseo de la Reforma

The stretch of the Paseo de la Reforma that runs south from the Alameda is lined with many of Mexico City's best-known landmarks, some of them occupying the roundabouts (*glorietas*) that interrupt the avenue at regular intervals. The first is Colón, the monument to Christopher Columbus; next comes Cuauhtémoc, the last Aztec ruler shaking his spear defiantly; then Independencia, better known as El Ángel for the winged victory atop its column; then the multicoloured glass pillars of a fountain illuminated at night; at the entrance to Chapultepec park, a fountain features Diana, Goddess of the Hunt.

The Monumento a la Revolución, resting-place of Pancho Villa

One block to the right of Colón, on Calle Ramírez, the **Monumento a la Revolución** (open Tues–Sun 9am–5pm) looms over the Plaza de la República, commemorating the movement in 1910 that paved the way for the modern state. The arched cube and dome, part of a legislature building never completed, was salvaged to become the shrine where Pancho Villa and other heroes are buried.

To the right of Cuauhtémoc, where Insurgentes crosses the Reforma, Calle Sullivan leads to the **Jardín del Arte**. On Sundays the garden blooms with paintings that artists display for sale; at night, it has become Mexico City's most renowned red-light district. To the left of the avenue is the worldly enclave of the **Zona Rosa**. Here, the streets are named after cities – though you might not recognise Amberes as Antwerp or Niza as Nice. If you need help, this district employs policemen whose badges identify the languages they speak. Pedestrian zones with pavement cafés go on for several blocks, lined with attractive boutiques, jewellery shops, chic restaurants and rousing nightclubs. There's a wonderfully cluttered labyrinth of handicraft and food stalls in the **Mercado Insurgentes** between Londres and Liverpool just off Florencia.

Bosque de Chapultepec

The wooded **Bosque de Chapultepec** (Chapultepec Park) spreads over some 400 hectares (1,000 acres) and, as one of the last natural areas in this congested valley, is known as the 'lungs of the city'. It was a royal retreat for the Aztec kings, who are believed to have planted some of the venerable *ahuehuete* trees (a kind of tall cypress) surrounding the hill at the park entrance. They also built an aqueduct to serve Tenochtitlán that ran down what is now Avenida Chapultepec. Chapultepec means 'Grasshopper Hill' in Náhuatl.

Fighting Pollution

Despite major steps taken to alleviate Mexico City's infamous smog (restricted driving, factory closings, emission-controlled buses and taxis), pollution persists, albeit at less severe levels than in the past. Mexico City sits in a bowl, surrounded by mountains. More than half of the country's industry and more than a fifth of its population is located in the surrounding area. In winter, a temperature inversion causes emissions, along with dust, to be trapped in the bowl's atmosphere.

For the visitor, dealing with the pollution is a matter of luck and perseverance. On some days you won't notice it; on other days it will make your nose run, your eyes water and your throat rasp. The best time to be outdoors or actively walking around is in the evenings, when the air is cooler and relatively clean, or on Sundays, when most factories are closed and traffic is relatively light. If you have respiratory problems, be very careful; the city's elevation makes matters even worse.

The hill has often played a central role in the city's history. Cortés fortified it and the Spanish viceroys built their residence, the **Castillo de Chapultepec** on its summit (open Tues–Sun 10am–5pm). This was being used as a military academy when the US troops of General Winfield Scott stormed the heights in 1847. The monument of six white columns at the base of the hill commemorates Los Niños Héroes, the 'boy heroes' – cadets who, rather than surrendering to

The Castillo de Chapultepec's epic historical mural by Siqueiros

the invaders, threw themselves off the castle to their deaths, one of them wrapped in the Mexican flag.

The Castillo became the palace of Maximilian, then the residence of a number of Mexican presidents. It has been the **Museo Nacional de Historia** since 1944. On the ground floor, portraits of leaders and summaries of their political fortunes may end up confusing even the most earnest history student. All the players in the pageant of Mexican history are assembled in a mural by Juan O'Gorman. Upstairs, David Alfaro Siqueiros does a masterful job of cramming a historical epic on nine walls of two rooms. In one, Porfirio Díaz sits with his foot on the laws; in another Emiliano Zapata reins in his galloping horse just short of the door.

Another ingenious, more easily comprehensible telling of the Mexico story awaits you in the **Caracol**, a snail-shaped glass museum tucked into the hillside, down from the castle entrance (open Tues–Fri 9am–7.30pm). Entering

Chapultepec Zoo (open Tues–Sun 9am–5pm) contains 2,000 animals of 260 species, half of them native to Mexico. The zoo is famous for its giant pandas, three of which were born and bred here, a record that is unique outside China.

at the top, you descend a spiral corridor lined with small historical dioramas from vice-regal days onward. There is a collection of remarkable photos of the 1910 Revolution.

On Sundays you'll think all of Mexico City's millions have turned out to picnic in the Bosque de Chapultepec, play ball with the children, row boats on the lakes or climb on a wooden horse to pose in a Pancho Villa-style sombrero for a park photographer. The shady walks are lined with food and drink stalls, balloon sellers and artists painting clown make-up on children's faces.

The President's residence is at the southern end, where an expressway divides the park. On the far side, an amusement park has dozens of rides, including a monster rollercoaster called the *montaña rusa* (Russian mountain). Nearby, you can see how the indefatigable Diego Rivera embellished the city waterworks with a mosaic sculpture-fountain of the rain god, Tláloc, spread-eagled in a basin and spurting water from every pore. Just outside the perimeter of the park is a wonderfully imaginative, hands-on children's museum, **Papalote Museo del Niño** (open Mon–Fri 9am–6pm, Thur eve 7pm–11pm, Sat–Sun 10am–7pm).

Museo Nacional de Antropología

The **Museo Nacional de Antropología** (National Anthropology Museum, open Tues–Sat 9am–7pm, Sun 9am–6pm) is not only by far the world's greatest collection of early Meso-American art, it is also a brilliant, unforgettable architectural masterpiece. A visit to this treasure house in the

Bosque de Chapultepec would alone make the trip to Mexico City memorable. The architect Pedro Ramírez Vazquez has used local stone and ancient motifs to create a most original modern setting that subtly evokes the past.

Guarding the entrance is a 4th-century BC statue of Tláloc, God of Rain. (When it was moved from its original location across the valley in the 1960s, thunder, lightning and rain broke over the city.) The museum is built around four sides of a court 82m (268ft) long that is open to the sky, reminiscent of the ceremonial spaces in pre-Conquest ruins. Overhanging the entrance to the court is an immense aluminium roof that seems to float without support, with sky visible on all sides. This canopy is pierced by a massive column that disappears through a hole. Perpetual 'rain' showers from this opening, forming a curtain around the column and the figures that cover it. Unseen above, a steel mast projecting from the column holds the roof

The Aztec Calendar Stone, one of the treasures of the museum

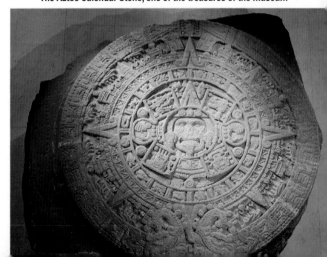

up by cables. The court radiates power, mystery and serenity.

A 20-minute multimedia show in a small amphitheatre beneath the reception hall traces the history of ancient Mexico and provides a good introduction to the museum. There is also a special orientation room for children and an excellent shop. The exhibition halls begin on the right and deal with the origins of the earlier settlers and the pre-Classic period up to about 700BC. The rooms are then devoted to specific groups and their sites – the Teotihuacán pyramid-builders, the Toltecs with one of their characteristic warrior-shaped temple columns and, in the great central hall, the Mexica, or Aztecs.

The Aztec hall is dominated by the huge, intricately carved Calendar Stone, discovered in 1790 under the zócalo. In its centre is the sun. Symbols represent the 18 months of 20 days, plus five 'unlucky' days, of the Aztec year. Rosettes mark the 52-year intervals initiating a new cycle, when temples were rebuilt or dedicated.

A particularly frightening statue of the earth goddess Coatlicue, with a serpent head and necklace of severed hands and heart, is counterbalanced by a serene representation of Xochipilli, lord of music and dancing, seated with legs crossed and face uplifted. Look for Moctezuma's iridescent feather headdress, a copy of the original sent by Cortés to Charles V.

> Though there are some English translations, most of the information in the Anthropology Museum is written in Spanish. An audio tour in English is available and an excellent guide to the museum is sold in the bookshop (on the left inside the main door). You can also hire an English-speaking guide: they'll be waiting just outside the entrance.

Next comes the Oaxaca room, with a Mixtec breastplate of gold, silver and turquoise and a reproduction of a Monte Albán tomb. The Gulf of Mexico room is noteworthy for its Olmec sculpture. Look for the outstanding small figure of a bearded man known as 'El Luchador', the wrestler. Here are beautifully carved jade objects from the ritual ball game called *yugos y hachas* (yokes and axes), the immense Olmec heads and a superb Huastec figure of a youth with his body 'tattooed' by bas-reliefs.

A masterpiece in the Aztec hall

The Maya room is equally fine. Among its many treasures are small terracotta figurines from Jaina near Campeche showing the costumes of Maya personages in minute detail; two magnificent portrait busts from Palenque; and stone stelae bearing reliefs of ceremonial scenes and Mayan hieroglyphics from Yaxchilán in the Chiapas rainforest. The remaining hall is dedicated to the appealing primitive art of northern and western Mexico.

Immediately above these halls, the upstairs museum illustrates the daily life of the descendants of each of these ancient peoples, or at least of the Indian communities now living in the same areas – Mayas above Mayas, Zapotecs and Mixtecs above the Oaxaca hall and so on. It is best to begin above the entrance and work around the courtyard anticlockwise, for the first room offers an introduction to the materials and methods of ethnology, the study of races. The costumes and

Life-and-death contest in the world's largest bullring

handicrafts of each tribe and photographs of their present-day environments are exhibited with life-size models of family groups.

The courtyard arrangement makes it easy to step outside at any point and find a bench for a little rest. Here you can read on the walls Spanish translations of Aztec poetry, surprisingly sensitive for a warrior race. There is a pleasant restaurant on the garden level. Ideally, however, you should not try to take in the whole museum in one visit.

Two other collections near where the Reforma enters Bosque de Chapultepec are worth a visit if you are not pressed for time. The **Museo de Arte Moderno** (open Tues–Sun 10am–5.30pm) exhibits Mexican painting and sculpture from the early 20th century to the present. The **Museo Rufino Tamayo** (open Tues–Sun 10am–6pm) is less a place to view this painter's work than another example of Mexican creativity in architecture. It includes Tamayo's collection of contemporary art from other countries. Tamayo, one of Mexico's greatest 20th century artists, died in June 1991.

South along Avenida Insurgentes

About midway along the Reforma between the Alameda and Bosque de Chapultepec (as the avenue skirts the Zona Rosa), you come to the broad Avenida Insurgentes Sur, another major thoroughfare, this one leading to many of the attractions on the south side of the capital. The first stop, a few blocks south of Reforma, is the Insurgentes Metro Station. This sunken circle shows how a necessary facility can be turned into a community asset. The plaza has shops, restaurants, book fairs, art exhibits and sometimes concerts.

Farther south, on the right at Calle Filadelfia, adjacent to the World Trade Center, an explosion of colour announces the **Polyforum Siqueiros** (open daily 10am–6pm, *son et lumière* shows Sat–Sun 10am, noon and 1.30pm). The crown-shaped arts centre is covered with David Alfaro Siqueiros's passionate images, and inside an auditorium houses the artist's immense three-dimensional mural, *The March of Humanity towards the Cosmos,* which you view from a moving platform. The 12-sided structure contains a theatre, café, exhibition galleries and a collection of works by the artist.

To the right of the next roundabout is the **Plaza México** – the world's largest bullring with 50,000 seats. The high season, from October to March, takes place during the off-season in Spain, so the world's top matadors are seen here. From June or July to September apprentice bullfighters (*novilleros*) take over to fight younger, smaller bulls (*novillos*) and the Sunday afternoon card is billed as a Novillada instead of a Corrida de Toros. The posters look the same, so be alert for the wording. Novilladas can be thrilling – after all, every matador has passed this way – but they can be quite dismal, too. At least the tickets are cheaper.

Many travel agencies include a bullfight in their Mexico City tours, which is a convenient way to get a ticket – you'll have a good seat along with transport to and from the ring. (Taxis are hard to find around the Plaza México after a bullfight.)

Farther down the Avenida Insurgentes Sur, still on the right, look for Diego Rivera's mosaic on the Teatro de los Insurgentes. Even here, Rivera is preaching politics.

Insurgentes next crosses into the suburb of **San Ángel**, once a village that the viceroys and élite of colonial Mexico favoured for their country houses. The metropolis has grown around and beyond the village and its surrounding orchards, leaving San Ángel a village within the city, an island of narrow, cobblestoned, up-and-down streets, attractive villas behind high walls and luxury boutiques. *Colectivos* to San Ángel run regularly from the Chapultepec metro station. They – or your taxi – can drop you off on Insurgentes Sur across the avenue from the **Iglesia y Convento de El Carmen** (the Church and Convent of El Carmen, open Tues–Sun 10am–4.45pm). The rooms of the convent are furnished with colonial antiques. Note the lovely tiled washbasins; less enchanting are the mummified nuns and priests exposed in the crypt.

From the convent it is a short walk up to the Plaza de San Jacinto. At number 23, there is a memorial tablet to Captain John O'Reilly and 70 ill-advised Irish members of the US Army's St Patrick Battalion who deserted General Scott's forces in 1847 to fight for Mexico. They were captured and hanged in this square. Among the Sheehans and Kellys note the unexpected name of one Herman Schmidt.

San Ángel is most fun to visit on a Saturday when the **Bazar del Sábado** on the Plaza de San Jacinto and a nearby *tianguis* (street market) are in full swing. The bazaar, open only on Saturday 9am–6pm, is a collection of superior handicraft, jewellery and dress shops tucked into corners around the courtyard of an old house. A buffet lunch is served in the patio, where musicians and fountains play. A pleasant walk up shady lanes brings you to the San Ángel Inn, probably the only restaurant in the world with its own

A mural by the prolific Diego Rivera, near San Ángel

chapel. It occupies the main building and gardens of a historic hacienda. (You can go in for a look or a drink without dining.) Across the street is the former home of Diego Rivera, now the **Museo Estudio Diego Rivera** (Diego Rivera Studio Museum, open Tues–Sun 10am–6pm). Among the collections are the papier-mâché skeletons and dolls that fascinated the prolific artist.

A little farther along, and turning east where Jose María Rico intersects with Insurgentes Sur, you come to **Coyoacán** ('Place of Coyotes', in Náhuatl), more accessible and less manicured than San Ángel. This neighbourhood has the atmosphere of an artist's colony – there are bookshops serving coffee, pavement cafés, a bandstand in the zócalo that looks like a carousel without the horses and a number of interesting craft shops near the 1583 Iglesia de San Juan Bautista.

Cortés lived here following the fall of Tenochtitlán, while the unhealthy ruins were being cleared of the dead

The kitchen in Frida Kahlo's house

and debris. His first wife died in the old Casa de la Malinche on Calle Higuera soon after her arrival from Cuba. Cortés was rumoured to have murdered her in order to be with his Indian mistress.

A few blocks from the centre of Coyoacán, you'll find the **Museo Frida Kahlo** (open Tues–Sun 10am– 6pm) behind a blue wall at Calle Londres 247, in the house where the artist lived with Diego Rivera. Kahlo's introspective canvases and self-portraits are full of the suffering she endured after a crippling accident. Her unmistakable image also appears in many of Rivera's murals. It's an interesting, idiosyncratic museum. Look for her collection of primitive *retablos* – one illustrates the escape of a grateful man who was cut down after being hanged.

Nearby at Calle Viena 45 is the fortified **house of Leon Trotsky**, now a museum (open Tues–Sun 10am–5pm) where his books, piles of clippings and a Russian typewriter are preserved just as he left them. The efforts this outcast Communist took to find safe refuge in Mexico were unavailing; an agent of Stalin split Trotsky's skull with an ice pick in 1940. He is buried in the garden.

Diego Rivera's personal collection of pre-Conquest art is in the **Anahuacalli**, a pseudo-temple on the outskirts of Coyoacán, built of black lava and designed by the artist (open Tues–Sun 10am–6pm). It is best visited by taxi or tour bus, since other transport is scarce. Among the treasures here are clay figurines with rings in their large noses from the west coast Nayarit people and a wonderfully alert, striped terracotta Colima dog once placed in a tomb to guide his dead master to the underworld.

Beyond San Ángel and Coyacán, Insurgentes Sur enters the Pedregal, a vast sheet of lava more than 3m (10ft) thick, now covered by a residential district and the **Ciudad Universitaria**, the campus of the national university of Mexico. The lava flowed from a small volcano around 450BC when the site was already inhabited. While quarrying building stone here at the turn of the century, engineers discovered skeletons and artifacts dating back to 1100BC. Some of these may be seen in tunnels in the lava at Copilco, an archaeological site off the avenue to the left.

The Ciudad Universitaria was founded in 1551 and is the oldest in the Americas, while its campus is one of the most modern. The complex, opened in 1954, shows why contemporary Mexican architecture has admirers worldwide. The 10-storey block on stilts encrusted with mosaics is the central library, designed by artist Juan O'Gorman. Murals and mosaics decorate almost every building. One of the most striking is the three-dimensional Siqueiros mural on the rectory, designed to be seen from cars moving along Insurgentes. Rivera's contribution is on the other side of the avenue, stone reliefs of Mexican sports from past and present on the Olympic Stadium.

> **The volcanic eruption that buried Copilco also covered Mexico's oldest complete pyramid, Cuicuilco, on the spot where the Avenida Insurgentes now crosses the Periférico. The structure – three concentric rings of baked clay and stone – had apparently been abandoned for centuries before being swallowed up by lava. A small museum (open daily 9am–5pm) displays various objects found on the site.**

A boating mariachi band in the floating gardens of Xochimilco

Xochimilco

Follow the Periférico ring road east from Insurgentes past the Ciudad Universitaria to reach **Xochimilco** and its famous **Floating Gardens**. All tour companies include a trip here. It can also be reached by a combination of Metro line 2 to Taxqueña and light rail (tram) to the Xochimilco station, from where you can walk or take the bus marked 'Embarcadero'.

In Aztec times, flowers, trees and vegetables were planted on artificial rafts of mud and reeds set afloat in Lago Texcoco. Eventually, these *chinampas* became anchored as roots reached the lake bottom. Indian market gardeners ferried their produce in canoes to sell on the canals of Tenochtitlán. Nowadays the gardens have blossomed into a sort of Mexican Venice: on flower-bedecked barges, boatmen pole festive groups or romantic couples through tree-lined waterways. Mariachi musicians on the docks board the barges or cruise the canals on boats of their own, coming alongside to play requests. Photographers implore passengers to immortalise the moment by posing beneath the floral arch with the barge's name – *Conchita* and *Lupita* seem to be favourites.

Time and growth have not been kind to Xochimilco. The town is still devoted to gardening and there is a marvellous flower market in the centre, where you can buy carved, painted canes and fresh fruit as well. But the canals are green with pollution and the bottleneck of taxis and buses around the plaza on Sundays seems to have taken root like the *chinampas*. It is not a tourist trap, however – most of the crowd is Mexican, many in family groups with picnics, and the music, hurly-burly and general commotion are authentic. Nearby, on the grounds of a former hacienda, is the **Museo Dolores Olmedo** (open Tues–Sun 10am–6pm) which showcases an outstanding collection of paintings by Diego Rivera and Frida Kahlo.

AROUND THE CAPITAL

The Pyramids of Teotihuacán

North of Mexico City, **Teotihuacán** and its pyramids are awe-inspiring. The city was built on an impressive scale two thousand years ago by an unknown race, and had been in ruins for more than 600 years when the Aztecs rediscovered it and called it 'the place where gods were born', reflecting the Aztecs' belief that the universe was created here.

This was the first great city of the western hemisphere, with a population of more than 200,000 and an area of 11 sq km (7 sq miles). At its zenith around AD500, the city counted more inhabitants than contemporary Rome could. Its style and symbols were copied by the Toltecs and Aztecs. It was a place of pilgrimage and trade, as evidenced by objects from all over Mexico found in its ruins. But it had no fortifications and presumably never recovered from an attack by barbarians who sacked and burned it around AD700. By the 16th century the city had become so covered by earth and vegetation that the Spaniards marched past without even seeing it.

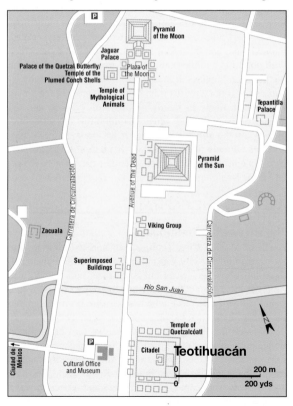

Teotihuacán is just over an hour's drive north of Mexico City. To travel here, leave the city on the northern end of Insurgentes and follow the highway to Pachuca. Buses for San Juan Teotihuacán depart from the Indios Verdes metro terminal and from the Central Norte de Autobuses. You can also hire a private taxi, at an hourly rate of about 90 pesos. The driver, who can generally double as a private guide, will take you here, wait for you and drive you

The impressive remains of Teotihuacán, once a mighty city

back, generally making for a full six- to eight-hour day. The ruins are open daily except Monday 8am–5pm.

At the entrance, a state-of-the-art museum with interactive exhibits provides an introduction to the site. Opened in 1995, it has in one part a glass floor on which visitors walk above models of the pyramids. Nearby, a small but exceptional bookstore offers a wide selection of books in various languages on Mexican history and archaeology. The museum opens on to the 39m (130ft) wide **Calzada de los Muertos** (Street of the Dead), the broad esplanade that ran 4km (2½ miles) from the Pirámide de la Luna (Pyramid of the Moon) at the north end to a still unexcavated point to the south. Straight ahead at the avenue's midpoint is the Ciudadela (citadel), a walled quadrangle with the **Templo de Quetzal-cóatl** (Temple of the Feathered Serpent) at the rear, along with a dozen ceremonial platforms on four sides. A staircase is flanked by heads of a serpent, whose body wriggles along

The Pyramid of the Sun once had a temple on the top

the base. Framed heads of the white-fanged deity and of the round-eyed rain god Tláloc as well as conch-shell designs cover the walls.

The Calzada de los Muertos is lined with stone temple foundations, all formed by a sloping skirt (*talud*) surmounted by a boxed mural panel (*tablero*), characteristic elements of Teotihuacán architecture. In the time of the Aztecs, these monuments were earth-covered mounds thought to be tombs – hence the street's name. It is, in fact, the grand aisle of an open-air cathedral, big enough to accommodate the scores of thousands who thronged here on sacred days.

The **Pirámide del Sol** (Pyramid of the Sun), on the right, served as the altar, rising 65m (210ft) on a base that is 221m (738ft) long on each side. Stand at the foot of the stairs and imagine the wonderment of the crowds looking up to the priests at the summit chanting to trumpets and drums. The sheer mass of the pyramid is overwhelming – an estimated

3.5 million tons of mud brick and stone, raised around AD100 by a workforce of thousands without the benefit of metal tools, work animals or the wheel. Originally, the pyramid and most of the other Teotihuacán monuments were covered with a thick layer of plaster. You can see from bits here and there that much of it was painted red. In this and other reconstructed archaeological sites throughout Mexico, the restored sections are indicated by a regular peppering of small stones in the cement.

A wood-and-thatch temple would originally have stood on the summit platform. The pyramid was built on top of a 300BC shrine and cave, which was thought to be the birthplace of the sun. Behind the pyramid and south of the citadel are geometrical grassy lumps that outline sections of the city still unexcavated.

The **Pirámide de la Luna** (Pyramid of the Moon) stands in its own plaza at the end of the ceremonial avenue. This pyramid is 45m (150ft) high, but since it is built on a rise, its summit is roughly even with that of the **Pirámide del Sol**. A number of palatial residences of priests or nobles have been discovered nearby. The **Palacio del Quetzalpapálotl** to the west has two elegant courtyards reached by a stair surmounted by a giant serpent's head. Carved reliefs on the columns of the lower patio represent a bird, the quetzal, and a butterfly. Discs of obsidian filled the now-vacant eyeholes and traces of red, green and blue colouring can be seen. The whole city must have glowed.

> **Visitors can climb to the top of the Pyramid of the Sun. The 247 steps are easier going up than coming down, because the steep pitch can instill a sense of vertigo. Persistent sellers of flutes and 'genuine' clay idols stake out the places where climbers stop to rest. The effort is rewarded by a sweeping view of the orderly plan and grandeur of Teotihuacán.**

A well-preserved fresco in the Palacio de los Jaguares

Teotihuacán is remarkable for its well-preserved murals. Jaguars adorn the walls of the **Palacio de los Jaguares** (Jaguar Palace), and the **Templo de Caracoles Emplumados** (Temple of the Feathered Shells) is decorated with parrots and conches. The liveliest and most extensive paintings are in the Tepantitla complex behind the Pirámide del Sol. In one scene, swimmers frolic in a lake. Another shows ball players with blue bats.

If you return to Mexico City on Highway 132D, you can make the short detour to **Acolman** to see the early Augustinian monastery, now a museum (open Tues–Sun 10am–5pm). Whenever you see a major church out in the middle of nowhere, you can bet that it was the site of an important Aztec temple. The monks first destroyed the heathen shrine, then replaced it with their own. This one is a good example of a church-fortress, built when the Indians were still considered a threat. It has medieval crenellation on the roof and a strong protective wall around the buildings. The cells and cloister still reflect the austerity of monastic life.

Puebla

The trip to **Puebla**, southeast of Mexico City, makes a memorable day's outing. Highway 190 from Mexico City climbs to 3,000m (10,000ft) through pines and upland meadows and descends through apple orchards, where you can stop to buy cider. Along the way, you get great close-up views of Popocatépetl and Iztaccíhuatl volcanoes. All of

Puebla is a national historical monument noted for its large historical centre containing many convents, churches and colonial mansions.

Puebla has been famous for centuries for ceramics craft called *talavera,* distinguished by polycromatic designs with blue, yellow and orange predominant. *Talavera* dinnerware and *azulejos* (tiles) are expensive but very popular. You will see the *azulejos* made in the *talavera* style all over Puebla on colonial façades, church domes and interiors, setting Puebla apart from all other colonial cities in Mexico.

The **cathedral** in Puebla is Mexico's second largest. It overlooks a shady zócalo lined with shops and cafés beneath the colonial arcades. To its left, on Avenida 5 Oriente, the **Biblioteca Palafoxiana** (Palafoxiana Library, open Tues–Sun 10am–4pm) in the former archbishop's palace contains interesting maps and manuscripts amid intricate panelling.

The Biblioteca Palafoxiana is the oldest library in the Americas

Across the zócalo and two blocks down the pedestrianised Calle 5 de Mayo, the church of Santo Domingo's **Capilla del Rosario** (Rosary Chapel) is Mexican Churrigueresque at its most dazzling. Every centimetre of this 17th-century jewel-box masterpiece is worked in gold-covered wood and plaster set off by a white stucco background. Wildly ornate carvings of cherubs and saints are lost in the foliage of a golden jungle.

Three blocks east of Santo Domingo is the **Mercado Parián**, a market of small shops selling onyx, embroidery and ceramics. Adjoining this market is the Barrio del Artista, a cobblestone street two blocks long bordered by a number of art galleries. Two other destinations in central Puebla are most entertaining. One is the **Museo Amparo**, the largest museum downtown (open Wed–Sun 10am–6pm), exhibiting a collection of pre-Columbian and colonial art. The other is the **Museo de Santa Monica** or 'hidden convent' on Avenida 18 Poniente (open Tues–Sun 10am–5pm), which operated clandestinely from 1857 to 1934 after it was supposedly closed by the anticlerical Reform Laws. Entry was through a concealed door in an adjoining house that led to two small cloisters and an upstairs gallery, where the nuns could peek into a church below. Policemen in the stationhouse next door

Chocolate Sauce

Puebla is the home of the famous *mole poblano*, the rich, spicy sauce said to have been invented by a nun during colonial times. *Mole* is, in fact, one of the most obvious Spanish-indigenous combinations on any menu. It can contain two dozen or more ingredients, including several kinds of chilis, as well as herbs, spices, tortilla, nuts and, most famously, chocolate. The sauce, served with chicken or the native turkey and accompanied with corn tortillas and rice, is often eaten at parties or wedding feasts.

must have been in on the secret – or singularly unobservant. The most interesting room is the kitchen, with a circular tile stove of delicate blue and white stars and flowers.

Ten minutes outside of Puebla, on the old highway 190 to Mexico City, is the town of **Cholula**, a very important religious centre in pre-Columbian times. In downtown Cholula, you'll find the largest pyramid by volume in the world. It remains unreconstructed and covered in vegetation. At first glimpse, you might think it a small hill, but if you climb the pyramid in front of it (also unrecon-

The volcano Popocatépetl smokes over the town of Cholula

structed) you will see clearly the outlines of a large four-tiered structure. There was a fifth tier, but the Spaniards replaced it with a church – Nuestra Señora de los Remedios. You can also walk through tunnels dug by archaeologists to explore the earlier stages of the pyramid's construction.

The pyramid was surrounded by hundreds of smaller pyramids, according to Cortés. On his march to Tenochtitlán he forestalled an ambush here by slaughtering thousands of the population and burning the temples. These were later covered by churches – there was supposed to be one for every day of the year. This may once have been true, but now there are 47, which is quite enough for a town of 20,000.

Just to the south of Cholula are two more churches which are famous for their beauty: **Santa María** in **Tonantzintla**, with its impressive Indian Baroque interior, which the writer R. Gordon Wasson interpreted as having several allusions to a secret native mushroom cult, and **San Francisco** in **Acatepec**, with its brightly coloured tile façade.

Cuernavaca and Taxco

Over the mountains south of Mexico City, **Cuernavaca** luxuriates in a setting drenched in colour. Blossoming flame trees, bougainvillea, hibiscus, camellias and poinsettia blaze along streets where jacarandas stand in blue pools of fallen petals. Because of the year-round spring climate, the affluent long ago picked the city for their winter homes – their red-roofed villas are hidden behind high walls. The 60-minute drive from the capital is along the toll expressway, Highway 95, or the parallel, prettier non-toll road, 95D. Buses from Mexico City leave for Cuernavaca every half hour from the Terminal de Autobuses del Sur.

The extravagant Baroque interior of Santa Maria, Tonantzintla

As you approach the town, you climb through pine woods and meadows, then drop to a plateau at 1,665m (5,460ft) from which Cuernavaca city looks out over the lush

Morelos Valley and back at the snow-capped volcanoes. All the land as far as the eye can see was once part of the domain granted to Cortés when he was given the title Marquis del Valle de Oaxaca by Charles V. After tearing down an Aztec pyramid temple for stone, the old campaigner built a fortress-palace for himself in about 1530. He not only introduced sheep, cattle and the silkworm but also Cuban sugar cane, which is still extensively grown in the valley.

Cortés built the palace in Cuernavaca, now a museum

The palace is now the **Museo de Cuauhnáhuac** – the Aztec name for the town ('place at the edge of the forest'), distorted by the Spaniards to Cuernavaca ('cow's horn'). The museum (open Tues–Sun 10am–5pm) contains cultural and historical exhibits, including relics of the original inhabitants. A highlight of the museum is a Diego Rivera mural of the valley's history, commissioned in 1928 by US Ambassador Dwight Morrow as a gift to Mexico. It depicts the conquerors lolling in hammocks while natives tote sugar cane, and repeats the often-painted scene of Spaniards burning Cuauhtémoc's feet in the vain attempt to force him to reveal the location of Moctezuma's treasure. Emiliano Zapata, the revolutionary hero who became famous for his battle cry of '*tierra y libertad*' ('land and liberty'), appears on his white horse.

The **cathedral** is set back from the bustle of the streets in a park-like corner. The crenellations on the roof proclaim it to be from the early 16th century, when churches doubled as strongholds. The interior is a surprise – under the old barrel

A beefy St Christopher in the cathedral at Cuernavaca

vault, the altar is an abstract modern construction, lit by sunbeams from high windows. Unconventional, too, is the rousing 'Mariachi mass' held every Sunday and accompanied by mariachi music, the traditional music of Mexico, rather than the more traditional organ. A refurbishing of the nave in 1967 uncovered 17th-century frescoes showing the martyrdom of San Felipe de Jesús, crucified in 1597 in Nagasaki, Japan, along with 25 Franciscan missionaries.

Across a courtyard, the Baroque façade of the **Capilla de la Tercera Orden** has the added charm of being adorned with naïve designs showing Indian men dancing, a reminder that Indian labour built these churches. The altar's retablo, the gilded, carved wooden screen, is notable. A band of blue talavera tile from Puebla around the walls enhances this attractive chapel.

A short walk up the Avenida Morelos leads to the **Casa Borda** and the **Jardín Borda** (open Tues–Sun 10am–5.30am). Once the magnificent villa of an 18th-century silver magnate, it was taken over by Emperor Maximilian as his private preserve in the mid-1800s, when it served as the setting for his romantic interludes with his lover, La India Bonita. The botanical gardens, complete with kiosks and an artificial lake, continue to flourish, and the front rooms house an art centre, Centro de Arte Jardín Borda. The gardens are a frequent venue for concerts and art exhibitions.

Cuernavaca has suffered in recent years – industrial development clouds the once-clear air, traffic clogs the downtown streets and the three connected plazas of the zócalo with their pavement cafés have become somewhat of a crowded bazaar. The old street market has been moved across the ravine that divides the city, a short walk behind and left of the Museo de Cuauhnáhuac. Although confined to an enclosure, the market is nevertheless bursting with vitality and overflowing with exotic produce, including an assortment of powders, leaves, bottled snakes and bark and roots guaranteed to cure everything from phlebitis to impotence. More of the same may be examined in the **Museo de Medicina Tradicional** (open daily 9am–5pm), in a house at 200 Calle Matamoros called 'la Casa del Olvido' ('House of Forgetfulness'), also said to have been used by Maximilian for trysts with his Mexican mistress.

> Cuernavaca's Pirámide de Teopanzolco (open daily 9am–6pm) was thought to be a hill until 1910, when the rebel Zapata mounted some artillery on it. The guns' recoil dug into the thin topsoil and revealed the building stone beneath.

Cuernavaca is known for its Spanish-language schools. Noteworthy, too, are the spas and thermal waters in and around the city. There are worthwhile short excursions to the attractive village of Tepoztlán and the archaeologically important hilltop ruins of Xochicalco dating from 200BC.

The drive to **Taxco** takes about an hour, part on Highway 95 to the coast and part on a pleasant winding road. About 20km (13 miles) before Taxco, a turn-off to Toluca on the right marked 'Grutas' leads to the **Grutas de Cacahuamilpa**, one of the most extensive cave systems in Mexico (open daily 10am–

5pm). Huge caverns 60m (200ft) high drip with stalactites and amazing limestone formations that run 70km (45 miles) underground. Guided tours take about an hour and a half.

The white walls, red roofs and flower-filled balconies of Taxco spill down a green hillside. The blue-and-yellow dome and twin pink spires of **Iglesia de Santa Prisca** provide the centrepiece of this picture-postcard scene, a longtime favourite with tourists. The whole town is a national monument. It was founded by Cortés to exploit Indian silver mines, but the richest desposits were discovered in the 18th century by José de la Borda. He became so wealthy that he built gardens and mansions and paid for the total reconstruction of Santa Prisca, explaining that 'God has given to Borda, now Borda gives to God'. The church's rosy façade practically writhes with spiral columns and twisted martyrs. Faces peer out of the stone at every angle. The ornate golden altar is worthy of this community of jewellers. You'll find their shops in every street and especially around the Plaza Borda, the sloping zócalo in front of the church.

Mines that honeycomb the hill beneath the town are still being worked – you'll hear the steam whistle when shifts change – but today the source of wealth is silver jewellery. An American, William Spratling, started it all when he came to Taxco in the 1930s, set up a silver workshop and taught local craftsmen to use ancient designs in modern products. The **Museo Guillermo Spratling** (open Tues–Sat 10am–5pm), just below the square, holds the American's fine collection of pre-Columbian art and features historical exhibits as well.

The fun in Taxco is to climb up and down the narrow streets, comparing prices and bargaining, and watching artisans cutting, filing and polishing silver, obsidian and semiprecious stones. Take a break on a restaurant balcony overlooking the square, from which descends a long stair-

Santa Prisca church is the jewel of picturesque Taxco

case lined with market stalls and food stands where you are served from steaming clay cauldrons. On Calle John F. Kennedy at the bottom, cabs and *colectivos* pass continually to take you back up the hill. From the heights of Monte Taxco, reached by a cable car, there's a great view over the town. Find a seat at sunset on one of the hotel terraces on the slopes overlooking Taxco to watch the sky turn pink behind Santa Prisca and the lights of the town spark like fireflies.

SILVER CITIES

For colonial atmosphere, the 'Silver Cities' are pure gold. The Spaniards never found the legendary city of El Dorado, but they did discover ore in the mountains northwest of Mexico City which poured out a river of silver for centuries and continue to make Mexico pre-eminent in world production. Throughout the 17th and 18th centuries, while Indians slaved in the mines, immensely rich mine-owners lavished fortunes on handsome cities literally built on silver. They embellished them with splendid churches, public buildings and stately mansions for themselves.

But these wealthy families were mostly *criollos*, born in Mexico of Spanish descent, and as such not entitled to hold the political offices reserved for the *peninsulares*, born in Spain. Early in the 19th century, *criollos* plotted to throw out the royalist *peninsulares* and for a time they made common cause with the oppressed Indians and *mestizos* of the mining towns. Thus the Silver Cities are known as the 'cradle of Mexican independence'. Now the charm of their picturesque streets and the mild climate act as draws for artists, retired folk and tourists alike – and with them have come attractive hostelries, shops and restaurants.

This region is easily accessible and makes for a great introduction to interior Mexico. Most travel agencies in

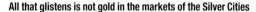

All that glistens is not gold in the markets of the Silver Cities

Mexico City offer organised tours of at least some of these cities, but a leisurely trip would be far more enjoyable. From the capital there is an excellent first-class bus service to any of these towns from the northern bus terminal, and a modern express toll road (Highway 57D) takes you directly to the closest, Querétaro, in three hours.

You can leave the highway just short of Querétaro to spend a pleasant hour in **San Juan del Río**, a trim, white colonial town where many shops sell opals mined from the region. About 12km (7½ miles) further on is **Tequisquiapan**, where hotels and public pools offer baths fed by radioactive hot springs, said to be good for arthritis. It's a popular spa, with good shops, riding and a golf course.

Querétaro

The outskirts of Querétaro are industrial, so press on to the historic centre of town and the **Plaza de Armas**, a beautiful little main square shaded by trimmed laurel trees and accessible by pedestrian-only streets. From here you can stroll in any direction and come upon stately colonial houses, exquisitely decorated Baroque churches and expansive convents. On the plaza is the **Casa de la Corregidora** (now the city hall). Here, in 1810, lived a heroine of the War of Independence known as 'la Corregidora' because, as wife of the Corregidor (city councillor), she risked her life to warn a group plotting revolt from Spain that their conspiracy had been uncovered by the government. Though locked in her room, she was still able to get a message out to the priest Miguel Hidalgo, who was to become the father of Mexico when he gave the cry for independence from his parish church in the nearby town of Dolores.

On the opposite side of the plaza is the **Casa de Ecala**, with its impressive 18th-century Baroque façade. Down Calle Madero is the **Templo de Santa Clara**, a church whose simple exterior conceals a stunningly complex Baroque interior. The altar screen is a masterpiece of carving and gilding. The Neptune fountain next to the church is by the great 18th-century architect Eduardo Tresguerras. A block south on Calle Allende is the former convent of San Agustín, completed in 1743 with an elaborate façade and a courtyard encrusted with sculptures in the late-Baroque style. Now it houses the **Museo de Arte de Querétaro** (State Art Museum, open Tues–Sun 11am–7pm).

The **Museo Regional** (open Tues–Sun 9am–8pm), on Calle Corregidora two blocks east of Santa Clara, occupies the magnificent former Franciscan convent and is worth a trip just to see the building. The museum holds a large collection of historical artifacts, including many items dating from the time when Maximilian was Mexico's emperor. His final defeat took place just outside Querétaro, and he was

The old centre of Querétaro has been declared a World Heritage Site

executed at the nearby **Cerro de las Campanas** (Hill of the Bells), where you will find a small Habsburg chapel. Two blocks north of the Museo is the Teatro de la República, a grand 19th-century theatre where a court met to decide Maximilian's fate.

San Miguel de Allende

San Miguel de Allende became rich as a market centre for the surrounding mining communities. The town, with a population of some 50,000, is special because it has kept its original appearance intact. It is the smallest and most relaxing of the silver cities. You come upon it from above and can look down on spires of pink stone, domes of bright majolica, white walls and red roof tiles. The whole, perfect ensemble is protected as a national monument. Cobblestone streets descend to the main square, called 'El Jardín' ('The Garden'), and a tour of the square quickly reveals that San Miguel has attracted a sizeable colony of *Yanqui* residents, at home in the pavement cafés, shops and restaurants. Many are students or dabblers at the Instituto Allende, an art and language school on the Avenida San Antonio, or the Bellas Artes Centro Cultural, in an 18th-century cloister at Calle Hernández Macías 75.

The influence of these schools may well be responsible for the profusion of sophisticated shops selling imaginatively designed jewellery and crafts in silver, tin, brass and glass. San Miguel de Allende has several interesting colonial monuments, but it's really a place for leisurely wandering, good shopping and candlelit dinners in cafés animated with Mexican music. Cosy hotels

> In colonial cities, you won't see stop signs at many intersections. Look instead for small signs with arrows on the corners of buildings. If the arrow is black, you have the right of way; if it is red, you must stop.

installed in old houses make San Miguel a good base for exploring the region. House-and-garden walking tours that give you a rare glimpse of the hidden opulence leave from the *biblioteca* (library) on Sunday mornings at 11.30.

The least expected building in this pretty colonial town is an 1880s Gothic-inspired church. **La Parroquia** is the work of a local mason and architect, Zeferino Gutiérrez, who took his inspiration from postcard images of French cathedrals. It is a source of great pride for residents

Don't miss the **Oratorio de San Felipe Neri**, a church built on a platform above the market and housing the tombs

La Parroquia in San Miguel de Allende

of the Conde de la Canal and his wife. The Canal family built grand houses in the town, but San Miguel's most famous son is Ignacio Allende, one of the heroes of the 1810 uprising for independence. San Miguel's name was extended to honour him. His house, just off the Jardín on Calle Cuna de Allende, is a museum furnished in period style.

Guanajuato

Guanajuato is capital of the state of the same name. The 90-minute drive west from San Miguel de Allende passes through the rolling plains of the fertile Bajío district. Guanajuato is tucked deep in the folds of a river gorge encircled by rounded hills. The topography defeats the grid pattern of most Mexican towns. Streets and alleys tumble down steep slopes and twist about among small irregular plazas. The houses, conforming to the hillsides they are built on, seem to have been thrown together in a jumble and are painted in softly glowing shades.

A baroque façade

Almost all have balconies overflowing with flowers and there's a competition in May for the prettiest.

Driving in town is hopeless; park in a hillside garage above the **Jardín de la Unión**, the hub of the city. Laurel trees grow entwined to shade this small plaza. Side-by-side across the street are the **Teatro Juárez**, a 1903 extravaganza in the French style dear to the dictator Porfirio Díaz, and the delicately decorated 18th-century pink stone **Templo de San Diego**.

Following this street leads up to the Plaza de la Paz, hemmed in by imposing mansions and the **Basílica de Nuestra Señora de Guanajuato**, one of the city's most impressive colonial monuments. The interior is neoclassical, with huge chandeliers and an altar to the Virgin, whose image was given by King Philip II of Spain. It stands, like the city, on a base of silver. Behind the church, the University of Guanajuato's white Moorish front looks old, but isn't. Next door is La Compañía, the church of the Jesuits who founded the university. The façade is one of the earliest examples of Mexican Baroque.

On the other side of the university, Calle Pocitos leads to

the **Museo del Pueblo de Guanajuato**, lodged in the palace of the Marqués de Rayas. The museum (open Tues–Sat 9am–6.30pm, Sun 10am–4pm) is mainly devoted to religious paintings. A more interesting landmark a bit farther down the street at number 67 is the house where Diego Rivera was born, in 1896. His evolution from these bourgeois beginnings into a revolutionary painter is documented in a small museum upstairs. Follow the street's ups and downs to the **Alhóndiga de Granaditas**. Guanajuato's royalists took refuge in this fortress-like granary in 1810 when the city was attacked by the undisciplined peasant army led by Father Hidalgo. When entrance to the fortress was finally gained, Father Hidalgo lost control of his peasant soldiers, who rushed in and hacked to death many of the people inside.

The massacre hurt the movement's chances for success by alienating many from the cause, and grieved Hidalgo sorely. When the tide later turned, the royalists took revenge by placing the heads of Hidalgo, Allende and two other independence leaders in small iron cages suspended from the four corners of the granary. The Alhóndiga is both a shrine to independence and a good museum featuring pre-Columbian

Cervantes Festival

In October and November Guanajuato hosts one of Mexico's most important cultural events, the International Cervantes Festival. It all began with traditional university student performances of short skits, (*entremeses*) by Cervantes, staged in the open air in the Plazuela San Roque off the Avenida Juarez. Now the three-week programme attracts orchestras, ballets, theatre groups, singers and chamber musicians, and includes a film festival and art exhibitions. Every theatre, hall, church and plaza in town is converted into performing space. Ticket and hotel reservations must be made many months in advance.

artifacts, regional crafts and costumes (open Tues–Sun 10am–2pm and 4–6pm, Sun 10am–3pm).

A block below, in the broad **Hidalgo market** you can get a good look at the different foodstuffs, garnishes and condiments that locals use in their cooking, including *tomatillos* (little green fruit with a papery skin used in sauces), brown tamarind pods, nopales, cactus paddles, mamey fruit, several kinds of avocados, the creased green and spiny *chayote* (the 'vegetable pear' that tastes like a delicate squash), fresh cilantro leaves and the *epazote* herb with spiky leaves.

The ornate doorway of the 18th-century Templo de San Diego

The grey-black ears of maize you may see are deformed by *huitlacoche*, a fungus prized for making a stuffing with a spicy mushroom flavour. Bright yellow squash blossoms are chopped and fried as filling for folded, toasted tortillas called *quesadillas*. You can sample fruit, buy herbal remedies, eat mummy-shaped nut candy and, on the balcony above, browse through handicraft stalls.

Following Avenida Juarez back towards the Jardín, you'll come to the Plazuela de los Angeles. Off this square is an alley, or rather a passage, so narrow that the flower-filled balconies almost touch. It's called the **Callejón del Beso**, the Alley of the Kiss. Guides – and any kid playing in the street becomes one at the sight of a foreigner – reel off a Romeo-and-Juliet yarn here about a rich merchant's daughter and poor boy from the mines who kissed across facing balconies.

The best views of the whole city can be taken in from a road that climbs the canyon walls and encircles the town, the **Carretera Panorámica**. On this road above the Jardín de la Unión is a stone statue of the brave El Pípila, the miner who tied a flagstone to his back for protection from enemy fire and crawled up to the door of La Alhóndiga and set it ablaze. It makes a good vantage point. The most macabre sight in Guanajuato is at the **Museo de las Momias**, the mummies museum, on the outskirts (open daily 9am–6.30pm). On display there are scores of naturally mummified cadavers propped up in glass cases. In Mexico, grave space is rented to families for fixed periods and then, unless more money is paid, the bones are exhumed and

Macabre mummified corpses in the Museo de las Momias

returned to the family to make room for other bodies. Because the bodies were preserved, there was little else that could be done with them.

A few kilometres out on the road to Dolores Hidalgo, the **Iglesia de la Valenciana** sits on top of what was the richest silver deposit in the world. The Valenciana mine made its owner fabulously rich and earned him the title Count of Valenciana. In gratitude, in 1788 he built a perfect gem of Mexican Baroque in pink stone dedicated to San Cayetano. Note the finely carved and painted features and robes of the figures on the gilded main altar, each a little masterpiece within the whirling, exalted whole.

Guanajuato's mines have produced more than a billion dollars worth of silver and are still at it. You can visit the mine and in the village find shops selling rock crystals and other minerals. Rock hounds won't want to miss the **Museo de Mineralogía** (Minerological Museum, open Mon–Fri 9am–6pm) in the school of mines on this road just above the city.

Zacatecas

Zacatecas, 325km (200 miles) north of Guanajuato, is in high, desolate terrain 2,500m (8,200ft) above sea level. For a panoramic view, take the cable car up to the **Cerro de la Bufa**, a craggy hill that dominates the centre of town. Looking out over the wild and barren land will make you feel as if you're on the frontier. From up here you can see at least three mines – this is mining country, and Zacatecas leads Mexico in the production of silver and several other metals. It was the large silver deposits that encouraged the conquistadors to found the town in 1546.

The city has the best preserved colonial historic centre in Mexico and, through civic pride, Zacatecans have gone to the trouble of burying power and phone cables to unclutter the urban views. It is a sheer delight to walk around here.

When you do, make sure you take in the façade of the **cathedral**. There is nothing like it in all of Mexico – its stone carving has so much depth and is so richly worked that no photograph does it justice. Other sights worth seeing are the **Museo Rafael Coronel** (open Thur–Tues 10am–5pm), a collection of native and folk masks from all over Mexico, and the **Museo Pedro Coronel** (open Fri–Wed 10am–5pm), with wonderful art works from the world over. If you're interested in seeing what put this little town on the map, take a tour of the **El Edén mine** (daily 10am–6pm), an abandoned shaft almost in the middle of town. For explanations in English, you can hire a tour guide for a trip around the city.

San Luis Potosí

The city of San Luis Potosí, two hours north of San Miguel, has grown more than any silver city, but you wouldn't be

The extraordinary carved façade of the cathedral in Zacatecas

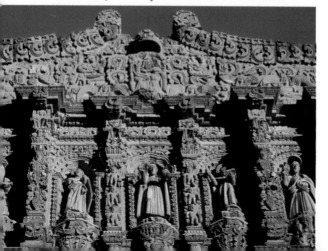

able to tell from the appearance of the historical centre of town. There, people congregate in the many beautiful plazas and pedestrian walkways that the city is known for, in much the same way as people do in any small town in Mexico. The biggest attractions are the Churrigueresque red stone **Templo del Carmen** and the **Museo de la Máscara** (National Mask Museum, open Tues–Fri 10am–2pm and 4–6pm, Sat–Sun 10am–4pm), with 1,500 masks used in Indian and religious festivals from every part of Mexico.

> Peyote, a spineless cactus with hallucinogenic properties, grows in the mountainous state of San Luis Potosí. It was used by the Aztecs and is still collected today by the Huichol Indians. Every year, Huichols embark on a six-week pilgrimage from their Nayarit homeland to San Luis Potosí to harvest the sacred plant.

The ghost town of **Real de Catorce**, an hour's drive to the north, was a boisterous mining community of 30,000 at the end of the 19th century. You can poke around its well-preserved ruins, empty shops, cantinas, a theatre and cock-fighting arena. Another place to go lies an hour to the east, **Xilitla**, where early last century a strange Englishman constructed modern-day ruins on a mountain in the forested Huasteca region of the state.

MICHOACÁN AND JALISCO

Michoacán and Jalisco, though neighbouring states, are quite different. Michoacán is known for its beautiful and dramatic landscapes, and for being host to millions of monarch butterflies that congregate yearly in a dazzling spectacle in the high mountains. It is the home of the Tarascan Indians, most of whom live around the highland lakes in the centre of the state. Jalisco is more arid than its neighbour and most of the land is used for ranching. It and its capital, Guadalajara, are the original home of many things Mexican, including *charros* (Mexican cowboys), the Jarabe Tapatío (Mexican hat dance), mariachi music and tequila. Guadalajara offers what may well be the best shopping in Mexico in its suburb of Tlaquepaque.

Morelia

Morelia, the capital of Michoacán, lies 300km (188 miles) west of Mexico City, about halfway to Guadalajara. It was founded by Spaniards under the first viceroy of Mexico and was meant to be a Spanish city. Its original name was Valladolid, after the city in Castile. The town was renamed after Independence to honour José María Morelos, who was born here and died for the cause. Most of the centre of town, including the cathedral, is built in the lovely brownish-pink stone for which the city is known. The layout was planned in

Monarchs on the Wing

Every year, from November to mid-March, a pageant of nature is held in a remote fir forest in the high mountains in eastern Michoacán. This is the winter nesting ground of millions of monarch butterflies, which migrate each year from as far north as Canada. The flutter of their wings turns the fir trees into an enchanted forest. February is the peak of the season, and it's far better if the weather is sunny. There are several day tours from Morelia; ask at any of the main hotels. These trips make for a long day. If you have a car you might want to make the trip in a leisurely fashion by overnighting in the lovely village of Angangueo and perhaps taking the waters at the thermal baths nearby. Take the old Highway 15 towards Mexico City; you'll see the turn-off to your left before the town of Zitcuaro. The main butterfly sanctuary, El Rosario, is open daily 9am–5pm Nov–Mar.

such a way as to set off the cathedral and principal churches to make the city appear more monumental.

Morelia's **cathedral**, like most Mexican cathedrals, is a mixture of different architectural styles; the beauty lies in how well these styles are integrated. In the case of this building, it is done to perfection. The setting is ideal: it is flanked on both sides by plazas and in front by a broad avenue (Avenida Madero); this allows views of the cathedral from a number of perspectives. Except for the sheer size of the building, nothing is meant to be showy. The façade is a model of digni-

The cathedral in Morelia blends baroque and neoclassical styles

fied restraint that harmonises a predominantly classical style with baroque and mannerist flourishes. The towers are beautifully proportioned to accentuate their height. The cathedral is best viewed in the late afternoon sunlight, which sets the reddish stone aglow. Inside you'll find a magnificent organ, said to be the largest in the western hemisphere; in May, the cathedral is the setting for the annual International Organ Festival.

In the immediate vicinity of the cathedral are a few blocks of buildings with stone arcade fronts, called *portales* in Spanish. Under the *portales* along the main street are cafés that in the evenings become popular places for conversation and socialising. On the same side of Avenida Madero as the pavement cafés, and in front of the cathedral, is the **Palacio de Gobierno**, a broad two-storey colonial building that was originally a seminary. Note the great simplicity of its exterior, typical of the architectural aesthetic of most of the city. Inside are murals by Alfredo Zalce portraying the progress of Mexican history.

One block along Madero in the opposite direction, the visitor finds the former church and convent of the Jesuits, now a beautiful public library. To the right of the library entrance is the tourist information office. The main entrance to the former convent, known as the **Palacio Clavijero** (open Mon–Sat 9am–6pm), is farther down this same side street. It is famous for its beautiful interior courtyard.

> **The Conservatorio Las Rosas**, on Madero, was the first music school ever founded in the Americas. The school is now best known for its boys' choir, the Niños Cantores de Morelia. Inside you can find out if there are any concerts scheduled during your stay.

On the street running behind the cathedral, diagonally opposite the Plaza de Armas, is the **Museo Regional de Michoacán** (open Tues–Sat 9am–7pm, Sun 9am–2pm), which covers the state's history in art from early pre-Columbian clay figurines to religious paintings from the colonial period. A block farther down that side street, in front of the baroque **Iglesia San Agustín**, are some *portales* that the city built to house food stalls in the evenings, where cooks wave morsels from their grills to tempt customers. Another evening sight is the illuminated Aqueduct of 253 arches that runs for 1½km (1 mile) right into town. The Tarascan fountain at the end of the aqueduct is also illuminated.

Three blocks east of the cathedral is the restored church and convent of **San Francisco**, one of the most beautiful buildings

The Palacio de Gobierno is housed in a former seminary

in town. The large plaza in front has been overrun by street vendors in the same way as the *portales* have. With its heavy buttressing and the cloister of small arches with Moorish elements, it looks more medieval than Renaissance. It is now the **Casa de las Artesanías del Estado** (open Tues–Sun 10am–8pm). Here you'll find the best of Michoacán's enchanting handicrafts. The first floor houses a museum and store with beautiful displays of craft work of all kinds. On the second floor are small shops, each representing one of Michoacán's craft villages. The museum and shops will give you a good idea of what to look for and how much to pay when you visit these villages, where you might see the artists at work.

Pátzcuaro

An hour's ride from Morelia in the direction of Guadalajara is the sweet, peaceful and picturesque town of **Pátzcuaro**, next to the highland lake of the same name. Pátzcuaro offers a sharp contrast in architectural style from Morelia. Here, the roofs are of tile and the walls are of adobe covered in stucco and painted white (with the lower portion painted in dark red, in the Indian tradition). The rooflines, the walls, the pavements – everything is slightly crooked, giving the town a lived-in, unassuming feel to it.

This town was founded by the first bishop of Michoacán, don Vasco de Quiroga, as the episcopal see of the diocese and as the state capital. He chose this place next to the lake because it was the heartland of the Tarascan Indians (properly called the Purépecha). To this day the Bishop remains fondly remembered by the Indians of the area, who use the sobriquet 'Tata' (grandfather) when referring to him.

Tata Vasco was already an elderly man when he arrived in Mexico. He was a learned follower of the ideas of Erasmus and Thomas More, who hoped to establish in this area a cooperative society of villages, each dedicated to a specific craft such as weaving, pottery, woodcarving or lacquerwork that would benefit the entire region. To this day, his allocation of crafts among the many lakeside villages remains intact, except that now most of the production is geared towards tourists rather than neighbouring villages.

The Purépecha Indians who inhabit this region speak a language unrelated to that of any other Indian group in Mexico, and closer to the language spoken by natives of Ecuador. Anthropologists are unable to account for such a migration, but this seems to be the case. In pre-Columbian times they were mainly farmers and fishermen, who defended their territory successfully against the Aztecs.

To get an idea of the different crafts to be found, visit the **Museo Regional de Artes Populares** (open Tues–Sat 9am–7pm, Sun 9am–3pm) and strike up a

conversation with any of the museum attendants, who are
from the area and have an intimate knowledge of the villages, then go to the **Casa de los Once Patios** (House of the
Eleven Patios, open daily 10am–7pm), a former Dominican
convent which now houses many handicraft shops. Also,
don't forget to visit the market, which is located in the Plaza
Chica and surrounding streets. The gigantic **Basílica Nuestra
Señora de la Salud** is an ambitious project that remains
unfinished to this day. On 8 December, the Feast of the
Immaculate Conception, elaborate celebrations take place
around the statue of Our Lady of Health.

Lago de Pátzcuaro, among the highest lakes in the world
at 2,200m (7,250ft), dominates the region. Green volcanic
mountains ring the lake and promontories burst from the surface to form three islands. Janitzio Island rises steeply to a
monumental statue of Morelos, raising a clenched fist up to

Typical red and white Pátzcuaro houses, with the Basílica beyond

The sun god disappears dramatically over Lago de Pátzcuaro

the sky. Morelos is always portrayed with the scarf he wrapped around his forehead to ease his chronic migraines. Boats run out to the island every 20 minutes or so from the dock on the outskirts of Pátzcuaro town.

All around the lake are villages in which virtually every house is a workshop. Santa Clara del Cobre is known for its copper; Quiroga for inlaid gold lacquerware; Tocuaro for its masks; San Jerónimo Purenchécuaro for embroidery; Jarácuaro for straw hats; San José de Gracia for its dark green pottery; and Ocumicho for grotesque animal figurines. The best Mexican guitars are made in Paracho. The town of Pátzcuaro produces woven fabrics; the Tarascan capital, Tzintzuntzan (pronounced *sin-SOON-san* and meaning 'Place of the Hummingbird') makes pottery.

From Pátzcuaro a scenic mountain drive of about an hour brings you down to the avocado orchards of **Uruapan**. The town is also famous for its hand-painted lacquerware. It is the ideal base for visiting the now-dormant baby volcano **Paricutín**. One day in 1943, a cornfield began to bubble and smoke; when it stopped nine years later, a 600m (2,000ft) cone covered the cornfield and a number of surrounding villages. You can see the tower of a church poking through the black lava field. Horses can be hired at Angahuan to visit the moonscape scene. Uruapan's lacquerware has floral designs on boxes and trays – perhaps inspired by the tranquil floral landscape now protected as Parque Nacional Eduardo Ruiz National, extending from the city limits to the Rio Cupatitzio and its waterfalls.

Celebrating the Dead

Chocolate skulls, sugar skeletons, coffin biscuits, bone-shaped bread. These are racked up by the millions for sale on the 1st and 2nd of November, when all Mexico observes the Día de los Muertos, or Day of the Dead. Far from being mournful, the holiday is a celebration, a time for visiting cemeteries and having picnics by the graves of departed relatives. Food, tequila, cigarettes and sweets are prepared as annual offerings for the departed and are placed beside family altars in the home on 1 November, All Saint's Day. Later, or on the 2nd, All Soul's Day, the dishes may be eaten at home or taken to the graveside and consumed in a party atmosphere.

The native religions of Mexico regarded life and death as two sides of the same coin, equally acceptable parts of human experience. After the Conquest, the Spaniards' fatalism and preoccupation with death, rooted as much in the deep Islamic influence in Spain as in medieval Catholicism, fitted neatly with the Indian temperament.

The Purépecha Indian celebration attracts many tourists to Lake Pátzcuaro. Many communities that ring the lake shore hold vigils in the cemetery all night to commune and honour their dead. If you wish to attend, you must make hotel reservations months in advance.

Guadalajara's Art Nouveau bandstand and imposing cathedral

Guadalajara

From Morelia, Pátzcuaro or Uruapan, the quickest way to Guadalajara is to drive north to the super toll Highway 15D. Both this road and the old Highway 15 pass by Lago Chapala, Mexico's largest lake, 83km (52 miles) long. Bordering its shores are a few towns with large populations of Americans and Canadians, such as Chapala, Ajijic (*ah-hee-HEEK*) and Jocotepec (*ho-ko-te-PEK*), artsy-craftsy communities that the expatriates have made their own.

An hour beyond the lake is Guadalajara, which Tapatíos (the nickname for Guadalajarans) call the 'The City of Roses'. It's a modern metropolis spread over a gently sloping plain at a comfortable 1,550m (5,000ft). With 5.5 million people, it is Mexico's second biggest city. To get at Guadalajara's special treasures, save time and energy by taking the inexpensive taxis and horse-drawn *calandrias*.

A good starting point is the colonial district around the **cathedral**. Begun in 1558 when northwestern Mexico was called Nueva Galicia, this imposing church is a blend of many styles, including rather un-Mexican gothic spires erected after an earthquake in 1848. The gothic interior is the cathedral's most impressive feature, and the painting of the Virgin above the sacristy door is said to be by Murillo.

Four spacious plazas that open the heart of the city for strolling flank the cathedral. On the south side is the town's main square, the **Plaza de Armas**, with an elaborate Art Nouveau bandstand made of wrought iron. Facing it is the 18th-century Palacio de Gobierno, a beautiful building inside and out. The central staircase provides a dramatic setting for José Clemente Orozco's masterpiece picturing an over-whelming Father Hidalgo avenging the sufferings of the poor with purificatory fire. The side panels, in Orozco's violent imagery, lampoon religion and depict the horrors of war.

On the opposite side of the cathedral from the Palacio de Gobierno is the **Museo Regional de Guadalajara** (open Tues–Sun 9am–5.45pm). The museum houses a large collection containing everything from fossils to archaeological artifacts, colonial painting to contemporary ethnography. Note the section on *charros*, the fancy-dress gentlemen cowboys – an extravagant *charro* costume is worn by mariachis. Jalisco is the epicentre of both these Mexican traditions. Behind the cathedral is the Teatro Degollado, built in the 1870s and recognisable by its Classic façade with statues of the muses adorning its portico. The interior of this theatre is beautiful. Check for concert schedules. Performances of the folkloric ballet (said to be one of the best in Mexico) take place every Sunday at noon.

Behind the theatre, a long, open-air mall called the Plaza Tapatía leads to the **Hospicio Cabañas** (open Tues–Sat 10am–6pm, Sun 10am–3pm), a former orphanage now housing a cultural centre. Its chapel walls are completely covered by powerful black and

Guadalajara is at its prettiest in March, when the jacarandas are flowering. However, the liveliest time of year is during the Fiestas de Octubre (October), when there are mariachis, charros, processions and fireworks every night.

grey Orozco murals expressing the artist's pain at man's cruelty to man. On the cupola overhead is his famous mural *Man of Fire*. (More of his best work, done between 1935 and 1939, is in the auditorium of the university on Avenida Juárez.) Around the corner from the Hospicio, the huge two-storey **Mercado Libertad** is the city's boisterous central market (daily 10am–8pm). Leather goods are a speciality here, particularly the *huarache* sandals of woven leather thongs.

But if you're serious about shopping, you can have no more pleasant experience than strolling down the pedestrianised Independencia of the nearby suburb of **San Pedro Tlaquepaque** (20 minutes from the centre by taxi). On this and other nearby streets are found the most sophisticated shops in Mexico, offering everything relating to arts, handicrafts, furniture and jewellery. Pottery is what Tlaquepaque was traditionally known for and it remains the most popular craft in the town. If you're interested in pottery, don't miss the Museo Regional de Cerámica and the Museo Pantaleón Panduro, showing masterworks of the potter's art. At the centre of the suburb (once a separate village) is **El Parián**, where at night you can enjoy great mariachi bands. Another village swallowed by the city, Tonalá, a bit farther east, is a very popular shopping place, especially for pottery, blown glass and wrought iron.

A very popular side trip from Guadalajara is a visit to one or more of the tequila distilleries in the nearby town of **Tequila**. The drive takes only an hour, but the

Modern statues recall the plumed serpent Quetzalcóatl

most enjoyable way of visiting the town is to take the Saturday train called the Tequila Express, which is operated by Guadalajara's Chamber of Commerce. Tequila tasting starts almost as soon as the train rolls out of the station.

THE PACIFIC COAST: MAZATLÁN TO ACAPULCO

Starting with the casual, sport-fishing port of Mazatlán, you can follow the coast south past charming Puerto Vallarta and down the exclusive Costa Alegre beyond Manzanillo, through laid-back Zihuatanejo to the dazzle of Acapulco. You're bound to find a place in the sun that's just right for you, and along the way travel through some spectacular tropical scenery.

Mazatlán

Mazatlán has long been famed for sport fishing and as the shrimp capital of the universe. Long-established clubs and modern hotels dot the beaches and golf courses, a modern marina and extensive tennis facilities add to the town's naturally inspired attractions. Despite the diversity of ways to enjoy time here, Mazatlán has yet to catch the attention of enough tourists to drive prices to the levels of other Pacific-coast resorts. This is good news for travellers looking for economy in a beach resort, for Mazatlán offers one of the top holiday values in Mexico.

Mazatlán's Carnival, first held in 1898, is the world's third largest Mardi Gras celebration, after those in Rio de Janeiro and New Orleans.

Although Mazatlán may not have reached pre-eminence as a resort, it is a city in its own right, with the largest port between Los Angeles and the Panama Canal and a population of nearly 500,000. There are elegant reminders of its history in the old downtown district – among them, the lovely **Teatro Ángela Peralta**, a national historic monument built between 1869 and 1874. Other sites of interest include the small but attractive **Museo Arqueológico de Mazatlán** (open Tues–Sun 10am–1pm and 4–7pm) and the **Acuario Mazatlán** (open daily 9.30am–6pm), a wonderful aquarium with adjoining botanical gardens.

Puerto Vallarta

Puerto Vallarta's appeal sneaks up on you – maybe it's the glimpse of a *burro* (donkey) loaded down with palm branches clopping alongside a taxi; maybe it's the sight of laughing children being photographed by their family on one of the waterfront public sculptures; or the glimpse of brilliant bougainvillea spilling over a balcony up a side street; or

Iguanas are common creatures in this region

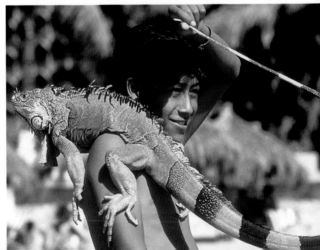

perhaps it's seeing one after another perfect sunsets meeting the expanse of blue bay from the vantage point of a *malecón* bar. No matter what it is that draws you in, no other place in Mexico so perfectly combines the gentle feeling of a traditional *pueblo* with the convenience and comforts of a sophisticated resort.

For those who choose, there is refined dining, plentiful taxis and an impressive collection of galleries showing an equally impressive selection of Latin American art. Or there are remote beaches with *palapa* restaurants whose owners personally bring in the catch of the day, challenging hikes to spectacular mountain waterfalls and diving to the tonal songs of seasonally migrating humpback whales. There are also organised city tours, animated booze cruises around the bay and a growing array of clubs with live music that ranges from mariachi to reggae.

On the beach at Puerto Vallarta

Puerto Vallarta, or Vall-arta, as regulars call it, is the most popular Pacific Coast resort. It is still small enough to charm, while having grown gently into its current size. It neatly divides itself into five key areas: knowing the particulars of each area helps you select a place to stay that best fits your preferences. Here's a rundown, from north to south: **Nuevo Vallarta** is actually located in a different state from the north, Nayarit, and has evolved into a sister destination of Puerto Vallarta. Ultra-modern ho-

Many places in Mexico celebrate the day of the Virgin of Guadalupe, with processions, fireworks and other religious and popular displays. Particularly beautiful is the celebration in Puerto Vallarta, which extends from 1 to 12 December, with nightly processions by different groups in the community. The Virgin of Guadalupe is the patron saint of this town, and the namesake of its famed church.

tels, many of them all-inclusive, front the wide stretch of beach here, giving a secluded sense of privacy. It is also the place to kayak in a lagoon or swim with dolphins.

Marina Vallarta is modern and sophisticated – a resort within a resort – with a championship golf course and exclusive marina filled with yachts and charter boats. This fashionable neighbourhood is a favourite with families and offers top-quality hotels plus abundant watersports, tennis, shopping, restaurants and nightlife. Along the **Hotel Zone**, wide, soft beaches front an ample mix of excellent hotels and offer a great place for recreational watersports. **Viejo Vallarta** is the signature cobblestone village extending to the north and south of the Cuale River. It is Mexico at its traditional best. From family-run beachfront hotels in the 'Zona Romántica' to eclectic inns that are poised on the surrounding hills, here

The Virgin of Guadalupe is venerated in San Sebastián

is where you feel the essence of Vallarta's charms, and is preferred by independent travellers and repeat visitors.

Extending from Conchas Chinas along the **South Shore**, the landscape changes to dramatic mountains that tumble towards the sea. Tucked into the private coves of this coast you'll find a collection of full-service hotels made to order for honeymoons and romantic escapes. At the end of this stretch of shore, you'll come to Mismaloya Bay, where you can still climb up the ridge to the ruins of the set built for the film *Night of the Iguana*. Ava Gardner played opposite Richard Burton in John Huston's film, but it was the romance between Burton and Elizabeth Taylor that got the headlines and started Hollywood's Vallarta vogue. The white houses and cobbled streets of downtown Vallarta are populated with restaurants, bars, boutiques, jewellery shops and art galleries. Buses and trucks roar through the centre on Highway 200 with a deafening clatter. A refreshing, shady retreat is Isla Río Cuale, an island found between bridges on the river. Birds twitter, men read the papers over a cup of coffee and a little girl plays with an iguana outside a shop that sells the same reptiles – though stuffed. Adjoining the upper bridge, the town market has a range of handicrafts on sale.

Cruise ships and sport-fishing boats dock at the marina north of town. From the marina, yachts cruise across the bay to **Yelapa**, **Las Ánimas** and **Quimixto**, a trio of isolated coves on the jungle edge and accessible only by sea.

The northern shore of Banderas Bay, about a 30-minute drive from Puerto Vallarta, is lined with some relatively undeveloped beaches, including Destiladeras, La Manzanilla and El Anclote. Also to the north, a new luxury resort development is under way, anchored by the Four Seasons and its adjacent Jack Nicklaus-designed golf course.

Traditional Mexican farming life goes its unhurried way just a little way out of Puerto Vallarta, up steep mountain roads to the east. **San Sebastián**, a 17th-century mining town, remains locked in time in its seclusion high in the Sierra Madre mountains. A day in this picturesque town, accessible by excursion bus or a brief flight, offers travellers a glimpse of life in another century and another state of mind. The simple and the sensational seem to coexist easily here.

Costa Alegre to Barra de Navidad

Travelling south along the coast between Puerto Vallarta and Manzanillo you'll pass through a stretch of extraordinary beaches. The 240km (145-mile) coast road, connecting tropical forests with dramatic cliff-lined coves, follows what is known as the Costa Alegre, or 'Happy Coast'. It's mostly an area of exclusive, privileged resorts, but also has some simpler beachfront places to stay. You come here for privacy, seclusion and immersion in nature, not for glitter or organised activities.

The loveliest section is the **Costa Careyes**, 120km (75 miles) north of Manzanillo. The few hotels and lavish villas scattered on the hillsides above a chain of little coves enjoy privacy and unparalleled views. The road rises and falls, twists and turns as it crosses ridge after jungle ridge, sloping steeply westward like the backs of great green animals leaning down to drink from the sea.

Barra de Navidad, a 16th-century Spanish base for Asian exploration, and **San Patricio-Melaque** are at opposite ends of a 5km (3-mile) beach backed by a lagoon. Both little towns have a languid atmosphere and inexpensive accommodation. A favourite way to spend the day is to walk the beach one way, savour some seafood at an outdoor restaurant, and take a shuttle bus back.

Manzanillo

Manzanillo, at the southern end of the Costa Alegre, has been around a long time. The harbour beneath the knob of the **Cerro de la Cruz** (Hill of the Cross) was used for ship-building and the Pacific trade in the 16th century. The string of beaches to the north, where mountains come down to the sea, have long welcomed a steady winter clientele who enjoy small, comfortable hotels and the chance to explore the countryside. But it was the construction of a dream-resort complex, **Las Hadas** ('the Fairies'), by the Bolivian tin multimillionaire Antinor Patiño that put Manzanillo on the jet-set map, especially after it was featured in the movie *10*. Las Hadas has spawned construction up and down the adjoining beaches; there are golf clubs, condominiums and villas and a strip of hotels, bars and restaurants.

The town of Manzanillo is undistinguished, except for delicious fresh shrimp and fish brought in from the working port. A sailfish tour-

Manzanillo fishing boats

nament is held in November and charter boats go out for other big game fish all year round. It also has a small but excellent archaeology museum, the **Museo Universitario de Arqueología** (open Tues–Sat 10am–2pm and 5–8pm, Sun 10am–1pm), which exhibits a collection of pre-hispanic artifacts. Shops seem overloaded with novelty T-shirts and curios made from shells, such as a truly curious Christ crucified on three clams. **Las Brisas** beach, closest to town, is broad and uncrowded. It leads to **Playa Azul**, **Las Hadas**, **Playa Santiago** and a succession of sheltered

A leisurely shoeshine in Manzanillo

coves. Pelicans and frigate birds, soaring champions of the Pacific, are endlessly fascinating as they patrol the shore.

Ixtapa-Zihuatanejo

When Puerto Vallarta began to become a household word, the avant-garde of beachcombing discovered **Zihuatanejo** (pronounced *see-wah-ta-NAY-ho*), a fishing village between Manzanillo and Acapulco. It had what they wanted: a sparkling bay divided into intimate beaches by outcrops of rock and wooded knolls, the simple pleasures of swimming and sunbathing and the freshest of fruit and seafood, not to mention cheap beer and rum. The secret didn't last long. FONATUR, the government agency that created Cancún, picked the area for its next venture, **Ixtapa** (*ees-TAH-pa*). Now the pair, only 10km (6 miles) apart but separated by the mountainous terrain, make an admirable double-act: Zihuatanejo for the charm of a village and its necklace of beaches, Ixtapa for manicured luxury on its own long beach, two good golf courses, tennis, windsurfing and all the amenities of a top resort without the traffic and hustle of an Acapulco. Its hotels are ultra-modern, designed to fit harmoniously into the tropical environment. Minibuses shuttle back and forth between the two towns, or you can rent a moped for independence.

Zihuatanejo has grown more sophisticated, with boutiques and candle-lit restaurants overlooking the bay, but fishermen still bring in their catch at the town dock. From here, you can take a boat out to the rocky point at **Las Gatas** – ideal for snorkelling and diving.

While Zihuatanejo is better known for its beaches and its fishing-village ambience, it has one of the better archaeological museums on Mexico's Pacific coast. The **Museo Arqueológico de la Costa Grande** (open Tues–Sun 10am–6pm) traces the history of this area from pre-hispanic times – when the place was known as Cihuatlán – through the colonial era. Most of the exhibits prove that the area was an important trading zone for centuries, with items from far-off cultures such as the Teotihuacan and Toltec.

Also worth visiting is **Barra de Potosí**, 45km (27 miles) south of Zihuatanejo, an idyllic fishing village surrounded by coconut and mango plantations, with a clutch of simple restaurants right on the beach. The social centre of Zihuatanejo is not a zócalo, as is the rule in most Mexican towns, but a basketball court. La Cancha is the gathering place where bands play on Sunday evenings and vendors offer *tamales* and *elotes* (corn), along with sweet, home-made popsicles flavoured with chocolate, cinnamon and vanilla.

Acapulco

For years, Acapulco was principally responsible for Mexico's attraction to international travellers. This is the kind of place for which the term 'jet set' was invented, the winter playground of the pampered. The publicity that follows the glamorous resulted in the city's growing popularity as a tourist resort and it currently attracts upwards of three million guests a year, the vast majority from within Mexico.

The first view of Acapulco coming in from the airport is of a sweeping bay, with white boats on blue water, a long curving beach lined with high-rise hotels and the city cradled in the arm of green hills. It looks like a large, rather unkempt city, almost incongruous as a beach resort. However, after the sun sets and the lights begin to sparkle, you understand why Acapulco still holds such an allure to travellers – the view at night is especially stunning. Acapulco's great

High-rise hotels right on the beach in Acapulco, Mexico's first resort

San Diego fort in Acapulco,
now a museum

bay was discovered in 1523 by one of Cortés's lieutenants sailing in a ship carried in pieces by Indians across the Tehuantepec isthmus. Later, galleons sailed to Acapulco from Manila, bringing porcelain, silks and ivory. To defend this treasure against pirates, the **Fuerte de San Diego** was built in 1617. Today the fort, between the yacht harbour and the zócalo, is a museum that traces the early history of the city (open Tues–Sun 11am–5pm).

There are some 20 beaches in the Acapulco area. The main strip in front of the big hotels facing the bay is about 11km (7 miles) long and quite broad, with room for the many sunbathers and siesta-takers. Few people swim along this stretch of beach, due to its reputed lack of cleanliness. If you do, be aware that there is a strong undertow at times: watch for the notice of swimming conditions posted at hotels.

Once the big beach was considered to be a series of beaches, still identified by bus stop signs along the six-lane main drag, **La Costera Miguel Alemán**. Now they have more or less merged into one. La Condesa is in the centre of the bay and at the heart of the hotel zone action. To its left is Playa Icacos and the navy base with its three-masted training ship; to the right are Morro, Hornitos and Hornos beaches and the harbour for yachts and deep-sea fishing boats. Hornos has restaurants and changing rooms and is backed by a public park. Beyond, the walkway of the Península de las

Playas closes the bay. Its beaches, Caleta, Caletilla and Angosta, are in coves with no surf. Launches from Caleta run regularly the short distance to La Roqueta island, where the swimming and diving is good from several beaches connected by paths through the woods. Older, smaller hotels and clusters of ageing villas mark this peninsula as the original centre of Acapulco tourism in the 1930s. Farther on are the cliffs of **La Quebrada**, world renowned for the divers who plunge from its heights into a narrow inlet.

From La Quebrada it's a short walk downhill to Acapulco's non-touristy zócalo area. The square is so overhung with trees that it's cool even at midday. It's backed by an Art Deco cathedral that began life as a cinema. Cafés flank two sides. You can buy a paper, have a coffee and people-watch people who aren't just more people-watchers. For a moment you might forget this is swinging Acapulco, but at night you'll be aware that a busy red-light district is nearby. Behind the zócalo, along Avenida Cuauhtémoc, is the working world of shops and dentists and bus stations for the million citizens who aren't on holiday.

The big hotels have pools with swim-up bars (which were invented here), tennis courts, water-skiing and parasailing off the beach, and more or less continuous

The famous divers of La Quebrada

entertainment – from beach and pool sports to Mexican music and dance festivals. At most there will be plenty of shopping on the premises and a choice of in-house restaurants serving Mexican or international cuisine. In town there are plenty of comfortable hotels with none of these extras, but very reasonable prices. They are found on the inland side of the Costera Miguel Alemán; just walk across the boulevard to swim.

Off the beach, Acapulco offers a lot to do. You can hop in a horse-drawn, balloon-draped *calandria* and clip-clop along to the Playa Condesa area's boutiques

Selling multicoloured *paréos* on the Playa Condesa

and the bars that have 'Happy Hour Now!' displayed at all hours. From the harbour, depart for any one of the many sunset cruises, swimming and dancing cruises, open-bar 'booze cruises', or glass-bottomed boat cruises. You can spend the afternoon on one of four golf courses, at a bullfight (Sundays only), in the jai-alai arena, or tearing down the Rio Papagayo in a jet boat. For children there's the **Parque Papagayo** (open daily 7am–9pm) with amusement rides; and the Centro Internacional de Convivencia Infantil (CICI, open daily 10am–6pm) has a wave pool, a giant slide and a dolphin show.

For next to nothing you can board one of the fuming, roaring buses and ride south along the coast, beyond the naval station, and over the ridge to Puerto Marqués. Here steep hillsides enclose a small bay and a beach solidly packed with open-air restaurants favoured by the locals. It could be a million miles from the sophisticated luxury just over the rise. To the north, half an hour past La Quebrada your bus or cab will reach Playa Pie de la Cuesta, where the mangrove-lined Laguna de Coyuca on the other side of the highway was the location for parts of the Rambo movies. Bird-watchers might enjoy a 'jungle cruise' on the launches waiting here.

It's after sundown that life begins for many in Acapulco, known for its nightlife as much as for anything else – nightclubs, discos, Mexican folklore, fiestas and stage shows (for some reason, cross-dressing acts are a favourite). Many of the night spots and restaurants are up on the hills, where you can feast on the harbour view along with the lobster. Along the Costera, fish taco stands and ice-cream shops are open all night long, along with a new offering of beachfront bars – a more casual alternative to the glitzy hillside clubs.

BAJA AND THE NORTHWEST

Separated from mainland Mexico by the Sea of Cortés, Baja (*Ba-ha*) is not quite Mexico. It is a curious mix of cultures, where the farthest point south, Cabo San Lucas, feels like a mere extension of the Southern Californian mindset just across its northern border. It is also a land of supreme contrasts and contradictions: most obvious are the emerald green golf courses appearing in desert landscapes and the luxury resorts rising in a land once known as a refuge for pirates and outlaws.

Baja defeated Cortés. He landed here in 1535 and later tried to implant a settlement, but this wasn't accomplished until a Franciscan mission was founded at Loreto in 1697. This was the first of a chain that was established nearly a century later up the coast in Alta California – as the present

US state was called under Mexican rule. Baja began its tourist life as a fisherman's secret, a place where Hollywood stars like John Wayne came in their private planes or yachts for fabulous catches of marlin and sailfish. Today, the secret is out – Baja is booming.

The 1,160km (726-mile) Highway 1 skirts the peninsula's arid mountainous spine to connect Tijuana in the north to the southern tip at Cabo San Lucas, linking the few important towns and crossing the Tropic of Cancer on the way. Airlines fly in from Canadian and US cities. Resort hotels and condos are in place on gorgeous beaches and more are being built. But with all these facilities Baja is still peaceful and unhurried, with a rugged sense of itself, and the beaches are still empty.

Baja South

➤ **Los Cabos** ('the Capes') is the collective name for three places: Cabo San Lucas, the original fishing port at the Baja's southern tip; San José del Cabo, a traditional town; and the 'Corridor', a spectacular 32km (20-mile) stretch of coast that runs between the two. This area is the principal lure of Baja, and how most people come to know this outpost extension of Mexico. Flying in, you'll see this is cactus country – more than 100 varieties are found here, from tiny buttons to saguaros 15m (50ft) tall, and the weird, looping boojum, found only on the peninsula.

San José del Cabo is a conventional town, increasingly gentrified to feel like a blossoming artist's colony. The hotel zone is set apart from the town right on the beach, offering plenty of privacy. The blissful quiet is broken only by the pounding of the surf and the cries of seabirds. San José's golf course is a green oasis in the desert, with angular peaks of brown mountains rising some 1,800m (6,000ft) as a backdrop. Lack of humidity in the air sharply etches every detail miles away, and this dryness keeps you comfortable even when temperatures climb.

At **Cabo San Lucas** you'll be besieged by boat captains who want to take you fishing. There are many kinds of craft for hire, from around 800 pesos per person for four sharing a power cruiser to half that price for a *panga,* a motorised skiff, including equipment and fishing licence. The deep-sea fishermen come back around lunchtime. Rare is the boat that doesn't fly at least one marlin pennant, and there's almost always a big fish being hung up on the dock to be weighed and photographed with its captor. To conserve the species, no boat is allowed to bring in more than two. Others caught must be released, though after putting up a fight for an hour and being gaffed, many of these do not survive for long.

They call these fishing grounds 'Marlin Alley', but there are an incredible 857 species of fish in the area. You'll see scores of varieties on the 10-minute glass-bottomed boat ride from the marina that takes you out to Los Arcos, where the blue Pacific slams into spray against pillars of granite as it mingles with the turquoise of the Sea of Cortés. Here, from a sand strip under eroded cliffs called Lover's Beach, you can snorkel in 30°C (86°F) water around the rocks where sealions doze and pelicans perch. Climb up a bit and scan the sea: a whirl of white water marks big fish chasing little ones; a marlin jumping seems to stand on his tail.

Scuba divers come to San Lucas to witness the phenomenon of the **Cascadas de Arena**, an underwater sand-fall carried by currents to a point where it pours in a stream over the edge of a trench 270m (900ft) deep. Diving gear and lessons are available at the marina, and the *pangas* or well-equipped dive boats can take you out to diving and fishing sites.

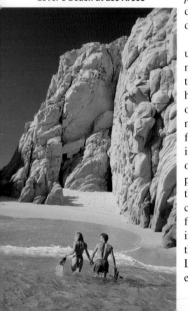

Lover's Beach at Los Arcos

Despite the wealth of natural attractions, it is the man-made golf courses that prove the prime draw to travellers here today. Six championship courses and one municipal course are open for play, with more planned, integrated into the new boom of luxury resorts. This high-priced accommodation, plus the fact that there's little agriculture in Baja and most foodstuffs must be shipped in, has resulted in higher-than-average prices in the Los Cabos area. Taxis are especially pricey – you should consider renting a car, if only for a day, if you are at all interested in exploring.

La Paz, on the Sea of Cortés, is served by international airlines and is a short hop from Los Cabos. Or you can make the trip on a four-hour bus ride through starkly barren mountains where buzzards ride the thermals above deep canyons. La Paz was once famed for its pearl

A mighty California Grey dives in the Laguna Ojo de Liebre

The Big Greys of Baja

For whale-watching, Baja California is unsurpassed. Every winter in December and January, some 15,000 California Grey whales arrive along the coast at the end of a 8,300km (5,000-mile) migration from the north. The females come to give birth and teach their calves how to come up for air in the warm, shallow waters of Baja lagoons. The Greys are up to 18m (60ft) long and the calves are 4½m (15ft) at birth. By March, after fattening on 190 litres (50 gallons) of milk a day, the calves are ready to make the long trip back north.

The main calving grounds are at Laguna Ojo de Liebre, also known as Scammon's Lagoon, about halfway up the peninsula – not an easy place to get to. Scammon was an American whaler who started the slaughter of the Greys that reduced their number to about 300 at the turn of the century. Now protected, they have made a strong comeback. You can see whales spouting and sounding in the open sea from Los Cabos. Or you can take a whale-watch boat tour from the marina. Boats sometimes come so close that you'll get a splashing from the flukes of diving whales.

fishing, described in John Steinbeck's novel *The Pearl*. But the oysters died out 50 years ago and La Paz slumbered in the sun until the Baja boom brought tourism. Some of the best diving and snorkelling is off the secluded beaches of Espíritu Santo island, a picnic day's sail from Pichilingue harbour.

La Paz claims to have the most sensational sunsets in the world – the sea turns shades of red and streaks of cloud ignite into flames as the sun disappears behind the dark purple bar across the bay. Patches of bright blue sky set off the livid clouds. The skyscape keeps changing until your film runs out, and then it gets even better.

Baja North

Tijuana used to be called 'Sin City', but many a sin has been legalised since the bad old days of US Prohibition, and 'TJ' today shapes up more as 'Sale City', if tourist statistics are a measure. Tijuana is the foreign city most visited by Americans, and most come to shop. They say that more traffic passes under the Freedom Arch at the California border than at any other crossing in the world: some 40 million trips a year. It's so easy – not even a Tourist Card is required if you're staying less than four days and not going farther than Ensenada.

Most of Baja California is a duty-free zone, so there are bargains on alcohol and imported luxuries, plus incredible rubbish that somebody must buy or it wouldn't be here. The full range of Mexico's colourful crafts is on sale here, too, in the government's Centro Artesanal and in shops along Avenida Revolución or in the modern shopping mall in the Río Tijuana section.

Not as frantic as in the 1920s perhaps, when the Hollywood crowd and half the US Navy from San Pedro-San Diego used to line up at 'the longest bar in the world'. But there are still superlatives: the margaritas come in pitchers, the food at countless restaurants is authentically Mexican and the nightclubs are as raunchy as you can get. There's plenty of sporting life out at the **Hipódromo Agua Caliente** where *galgos* (greyhounds) race nightly at 7.45pm and Saturday and Sunday at 2pm. Bullfights are scheduled every Sunday from May to September in two rings.

The face of the new, commercial Tijuana, the fourth-largest city in Mexico, is presented by the fast-growing factories where low-cost Mexican labour assembles electronic products, and by the lively cultural centre on the river, where there's always a fiesta of Mexican music and dance. But you don't have to look far to find the old face of Sin City still leering underneath the cosmetic clean-up.

The tollway south, Highway 1, quickly brings you to more sedate **Ensenada**, the long-established resort and fishing town on Todos Santos Bay, also Baja's busiest port. The drive down the cliff-lined coast is exhilarating, and you can stop to look for migrating whales, which navigate along the

On the coast road to Ensenada

shore in December and January. In summer, watch the surfers. East of Tijuana is a rich agricultural area and the state's capital, Mexicali and its California counterpart, Caléxico. The border crossing here leads to San Felipe at the top of the Sea of Cortés. Tides here drop 10m (30ft), compared to 1m (3ft) at Los Cabos. It's a weekend hangout for dune-buggy stunt drivers.

Copper Canyon

La Barranca del Cobre ('Copper Canyon') is one face of Mexico most visitors never see, but those who do never forget it. Much of the fun is getting here, thanks to the **Chihuahua al Pacífico railway**, which connects Chihuahua City to the coastal city of Los Mochis in the state of Sinaloa. It is nothing short of a spectacular ride – one of the great train journeys of the world. The single-track line climbs 2,450m (8,000ft) to the rim of Copper Canyon. Along the way, the train passes through 86 tunnels and over 39 bridges, an engineering feat begun in 1898 by an American entrepreneur as part of his quixotic dream of linking Kansas City to the Pacific Ocean. Sixty-three years and $100 million later it was completed by the Mexican government.

It's best to go from Los Mochis so that you see the most amazing scenery (between El Fuerte and Bahuichivo) in full daylight. The first-class train makes the 672km (420-mile) trip in about 14 hours, which includes a 15-minute stop at **Divisadero** on the rim of the canyon, allowing passengers to look down into the junction of three gorges more than 1,200m (4,000ft) deep. But to see more of the canyon area requires an overnight stay in **Divisa-**

> **'Copper Canyon' is actually a vast network of canyons cutting into the Sierra Tarahumara. In area, it is four times as large as the Grand Canyon in Colorado.**

Pausing to take in the stupendous views in Copper Canyon

dero/Barrancas or in one of the other two principal stops in the canyon area: **Creel** and **Bahuichivo/Cerocahui**. At any of these towns you can find guides to take you hiking or horse-riding into the canyons or along the rim, or make a side-trip by car to one of the old silver-mining towns to be found at the bottom of the canyons. If you're going to stay at one of these towns, you should make reservations, because hotel rooms are few in number. The busiest times of year here are March and October to early November.

At any of the stops you make in the area, you'll find yourself in wild and beautiful canyon land with stunning mountain vistas, sheer rock walls and strangely shaped rock formations. There's a tremendous variety of flora and fauna, too. Up at the top, in the rim country, pine forests predominate, while in the canyons the climate is subtropical, with many species of tropical trees, bushes, cacti and wildlife. The region has several waterfalls, including **Basaseachic**,

> The running prowess and endurance of the Tarahumara are legendary. It is said that they can outrun a deer, and they think nothing of crossing a canyon or two on foot just to pay a visit to a friend.

the tallest single cascade in North America.

This is also the land of the Tarahumara Indians. Numbering some 50,000, they live in small settlements scattered about the region. These Indians observe elaborate rules of courtesy among themselves, which leads observers to call them shy. Those Tarahumara who deal regularly with tourists, however, have learned the ways of the outside world. Some Tarahumara women have little stands at Divisadero where they sell handicrafts, including pine-needle baskets, wood carvings and musical instruments, but you'll see the Tarahumara at any of the towns in these mountains.

Chihuahua

Chihuahua is a busy city of 1.5 million people, a five-hour drive south of El Paso, Texas. It was **Pancho Villa's** headquarters and the house where his widow lived until 1981 is now the **Museo de la Revolución** (open Tues–Sat 9am–1pm and 3–7pm, Sun 9am–5pm). The best way to see this museum is with a local guide who will know all the stories about the fascinating life of Pancho Villa and his 23 wives, and can provide some context to what you see here. Included in the collection is the 1922 open Dodge sedan in which Villa was ambushed, and photos of him and his favourite troops sporting bandoliers and looking like bad *hombres*. Villa's grave is in Chihuahua, but it is empty. When he was reburied in the Revolution Monument in Mexico City, his body was found without a head – no one knows why.

The **Museo Quinta Gameros** (open Tues–Sun 11am–2pm and 4–7pm) is housed in a stunning mansion that provides the setting for a large collection of Mexican Art Nouveau furniture, which was brought from Mexico City. If you're a history buff, you may want to visit the **Calabozo de Miguel Hidalgo** (Hidalgo's dungeon, open Tues–Sun 9am–6pm), where the Father of Mexican Independence was held prisoner until he was executed nearby, at a spot where the **Palacio de Gobierno** now stands (also worth a visit for the building's architecture and murals – open daily 8am–10pm).

THE YUCATÁN

The Yucatán is different from the rest of Mexico. Where all is mountainous elsewhere, the Yucatán is flat as a tortilla, a piece of the ocean floor pushed upward between the Gulf of Mexico and the Caribbean millions of years ago. This limestone slab is porous, quickly absorbing rainfall. Water percolates into the porous limestone, forming underground

The Pyramid of Kukulcán at Chichén Itzá

caverns and rivers. When the roofs of these caverns collapse, the water is exposed in the well-like formations called *cenotes*. The many *cenotes* in the area were very important to the Maya and, more than 2,000 years ago became focal points for their communities, of which there were hundreds. Uxmal and Chichén Itzá have been the most extensively excavated.

In colonial times, this region far away from the viceroy's capital in Mexico City had its own governor. When Mexico gained independence, the Yucatán became an independent country and remained that way for two years. Then it decided to join Mexico, but in the political chaos of the following years, opted for independence again in 1846. The landowners, fearing an invasion force, armed their Mayan peasants, who promptly turned their weapons on their oppressors. This

Hanging by a Thread

For residents of the Yucatán, hammocks are what beds are for us. Yucatecans will sleep in them all night long and complain when they are forced to sleep in a bed. Because Yucatecan net hammocks do such a good job of distributing weight, they are more comfortable than the canvas hammocks commonly found elsewhere. But how do you measure the quality of a net hammock? Width would be a good way, but for the fact that these hammocks can be stretched as wide as you want. Weight is a better measure. A hammock that weighs about 1.5kg (about 3½ lb) is thought to be of good quality. If you get a lighter hammock, by the time you have stretched it out wide enough to lie across it diagonally (which is how you are supposed to sleep in them), the threads are so far apart that you can feel them against your skin. The knitted part of the hammock should be of fine cotton thread and be at least 2m (6ft) long. The general rule is that the finer and the more numerous the threads, the more expensive the hammock.

struggle to wipe out the European population from the peninsula is known in history as the Caste War. The Maya were almost successful; they were later defeated, but managed to keep de facto control of the remote eastern part of the peninsula well into the 20th century.

In the 1870s, the fortunes of the peninsula rose again with the *henequen* boom. *Henequen*, a fibre harvested from a species of agave plant, was used to make cordage and was in great demand before the invention of synthetic fibres. *Henequen* production grew dramatically up until the Mexican Revolution, from which the

Henequen is still cultivated in the Yucatán

industry never fully recovered. It wasn't until the 1970s that the Yucatán boomed again. This time fortunes came in the form of tourism, which began with the development of Cancún, now the most popular resort in Mexico.

Mérida

Mérida, in the heart of the Yucatán, has been the most important city on the peninsula ever since its founding in 1541. It is a charming city of tropical, pastel-coloured colonial buildings and grand 19th-century mansions. You can tour it in charming fashion, too, by open bus or horse-drawn carriage. There is a lively street scene here in the evenings, when the city's inhabitants stroll about visiting friends. Small shaded plazas with outdoor cafés provide popular places for people to congregate, and the main square is never empty. Besides strolling about, there is always something cooking in this town. Every night there is some dance performance or concert; most of these are free. To find out what's available, ask at your hotel or one of the tourism offices. Every Sunday, the city closes off a section of streets and plazas to hold a weekly fiesta called **Mérida en Domingo**, with concerts, comedy performances, food stalls, a flea market and a book market, among other things. Later in the evening, a band plays mambos and rumbas in front of the town hall, and people come to dance in the street.

Mérida's 16th-century cathedral, the oldest in Mexico

Other pleasures include restaurants, museums, some interesting night clubs and the best shopping in all the Yucatán. Items to shop for include locally made *hamacas* (hammocks) and *guayaberas* (the traditional loose-fitting shirt worn in tropical Spanish-speaking countries in place of a suit), which can be found at a number of specialist outlets around the Plaza Grande and neighbouring streets. The place to buy Panama-style hats, made from finely woven fibres of the *jipi* palm, and *huipils*, heavily embroidered cotton tunics worn by native

Yucatecan women, is the handicrafts market, a couple of blocks southeast of the Plaza Grande.

The old heart of Mérida is the main square, the **Plaza Grande**. On the east side is the oldest **cathedral** in Mexico, which celebrated its 400th anniversary in 1998. It is an impressive structure devoid of elaborate decoration and most of its stucco has fallen off, exposing the bare rock of the walls. If the cathedral reminds you of a fortress, the

The courtyard of the
Palacio Montejo

resemblance is not without reason – it was built in the days of sporadic revolts by the region's Maya Indians. The interior is even more bare, thanks to its having been sacked in 1915 during the Mexican Revolution.

The former archbishop's palace, beside the cathedral, now houses the **Museo Macay** (Musuem of Contemporary Art, open Wed–Sun 10am–5pm). On the south side of the plaza is the **Palacio Montejo**, where the Montejos, the conquistadors of the region, lived. It is a lovely building with heavy Plateresque ornamentation, now occupied by a bank. Descendants of the Montejos lived in the house until the 1970s. Across the plaza from the cathedral is the **Ayuntamiento** (town hall), and on the remaining side of the square is the **Palacio de Gobierno** (Governor's Palace, open daily 8am–10pm). Go inside and you will see some extravagant murals by a famous local artist, Fernando Castro Pacheco.

During Mérida's heyday, from 1880 to 1910, millionaire *henequen* planters built their mansions on the **Paseo Montejo**, Mérida's own Champs Élysées. Today, most of the boulevard is occupied by banks, airline offices and fashionable restaurants. Of the old mansions that remain standing, one of the finest is the **Palacio Cantón Rosado**, now housing a wonderful **anthropology museum** (open Tues–Sat 9am–8pm, Sun 8am–2pm) which can help you make sense of what you see when you go out to the ruins. Look for the explanation of Mayan numbers, a bar and dot system, and the exhibit showing how the heads of infants were deformed by binding them between two boards to produce sloping foreheads. To meet Mayan beauty standards, teeth were filed and eyes made cross-eyed by dangling a bead before them.

From Mérida, you have a choice of many side trips. There are several old *henequen* haciendas that have been restored into museum-restaurants or hotels. These are lovely places, perfect for those looking for a peaceful getaway. Less than an hour east of Mérida is **Izamal**, a quiet town where the *calesa* (horse-drawn carriage) is the most common form of taxi and the attractions include the 16th-century **Monastery of San Antonio de Padua**, and **Kinich Kakmo**, the largest of several ancient Mayan pyramids dotted around town. Just northwest of Mérida is **Dzibichaltún**, the ruins of a small Mayan city, with a small museum on site. Beyond the ruins but still not far from Mérida is the port of **Progreso**, where Meridianos like to go to the beach. Due west of Mérida is **Celestún**,

Flamingos breed at Celestún

from where you can hire a boat to visit the flamingo colony in the **Celestún Wildlife Refuge**. As well as flamingos, many other bird species thrive here. South of Mérida, an hour and a half away, is the famous Maya city of Uxmal and, nearby, the other ruins that are part of the Puuc Route.

Uxmal

The road to **Uxmal** (pronounced *Oosh-mal*), 82km (50 miles) south of Mérida, goes through Yucatán's low scrub thickets and past some fields of agave. En route, at **Yaxcopoil** you can visit a 17th-century hacienda mus-

The Pyramid of Adivino in Uxmal

eum to see how the planters lived and the way *henequen* fibre is extracted from the agave. The curious little sacks hanging in trees along the way are black oriole nests.

The Uxmal ruins are the finest examples of a Mayan style called Puuc (pronounced *pook*), named after the low Puuc hills of this district. It is characterised by rectangular buildings, square columns and an upper frieze panel decorated with intricate projecting geometrical mosaics. Many panels are covered with masks of the rain god Chaac, an ugly fellow with a curling trunk snout and swirly eyes. You'll notice these upper sections are slightly angled outwards. The Mayans never mastered the true arch, but came close with the pointed corbel arch of overlapping stones. Lintels over some doorways are made of the original sapodilla wood (one of them carbon-dated to AD569). This wood is so heavy it doesn't float in water.

Straight ahead as you enter the ruins is the **Pirámide del Adivino** (Pyramid of the Magician). The pyramid, with rounded corners, was built in stages between AD600 and 900, each stage covering the preceding one. The path from the entrance passes a *chultún* (cistern) to collect rain, the only source of water in this area, which has no *cenotes*. Consequently, the rain god was the all-important deity. Approach the steep three-tiered pyramid from the rear and climb 120 steps to the top. (There is a safety chain you can hang on to for the climb – just don't look back.) Moving round to the front side, you'll see many Chaac masks on the corners of the temple doorway. The door itself is the mouth of a giant mask. From this vantage point you'll see the other principal ruins spread out beneath you and many other still unexcavated mounds in the thick brush beyond.

The so-called 'Nunnery'

Directly in front is the **Cuadrángulo de las Monjas** (Nunnery) – incidentally, names given to Mayan ruins are usually pure conjecture, and no one really knows the purpose of many of their structures. The grassy quadrangle is enclosed by four stately low buildings on different levels. On the east, the upper panel of latticework mosaic is decorated with inverted pyramids formed by double-headed serpent bars. The west-side frieze has a stylised snake weaving through it from right to left.

There's a feather canopy crowning a throne above the central door, where the face of an old man with a turtle body can be seen. Niches in the façade represent palm-thatched houses. This theme is repeated over the doorways

Stone mask of the god Itzqamná in the Nunnery Quadrangle

on the south building, where 16 rooms may have been a kind of inn for priests on pilgrimages to Uxmal. Head south through a corbel arch and follow a path through the **Juego de Pelota** (Ball Court) to the **Palomar** (Dovecote), so called because of the pierced triangular elements of its roof-comb. It is just one wall of a large, unreconstructed complex to the south.

Rubble on three unrestored sides of the **Gran Pirámide** (Great Pyramid) suggests that the Mayans were covering it to build a larger one when Uxmal was abandoned around AD1000. A small building, rather Grecian in its harmonious proportions, stands between the pyramid and the ball court. The stone tortoises (*tortugas*) decorating its upper frieze have earned it the name **Casa de las Tortugas** and it carries the symbolism of fertility and rain.

Continue on to the field fronting the imposing **Palacio del Gobernador** (Governor's Palace). The entire area is a man-made platform. From a distance you'll be able to see that among the thousands of stones making up the façade (all cut without metal tools and fitted without mortar), projecting Chaac heads form an undulating serpent. The fallen column in the plaza is thought to have been used in astronomical observations. There are other partially restored ruins beyond this platform. The Casa de la Vieja (House of the Old Woman) is supposed to be the temple of a sorceress who, with her dwarf grandson, the Magician, tricked the king of Uxmal and became rulers of the city. Nearby is a building with phallic drainpipes. Beyond the Dovecote a path leads to the Grupo del Cementerio, a cemetery complex where platforms have skull and crossbones reliefs.

Uxmal's grounds are open daily 8am–5pm. A 45-minute sound-and-light show in Spanish starts at 8pm, and is repeated in English at 9pm. The dramatised history tells the story of how Uxmal declined because of successive failures of Chaac to deliver the rains and, finally, as the result of a war that shifted power to other cities. Within an hour's drive of Uxmal are four other interesting Mayan cities: Kabah, Sayil, Xlapak and Labná. Paved Mayan roads once connected all four cities.

Campeche

About three hours southwest of Mérida off Route 180 is **Campeche**, a Gulf of Mexico port and the capital of the state bearing the same name. Here, as everywhere along the gulf side of the peninsula, the water isn't as clear and blue as it is on the Caribbean side; as a result, few tourists come here, and those who do are usually on their way from Mérida to Palenque or to the Río Bec region. Even so, the city is well worth a visit, a beautiful example of a lowland colonial town.

In the 17th century, Campechanos constructed a high wall around their city with four gates and several bastions (*baluartes*) as fortifications against marauding pirates who had already captured and sacked the town twice before. They also built **forts** on each of the two hills above the town. Now most of the wall is gone, except for two sections bordering the seaward and landward gates, which are quite impressive. On Friday and Saturday nights, there's an entertaining **sound-and-light show**, illustrating the history of Campeche, at the landward gate. The bastions are now used for a variety of purposes from the City Museum (Baluarte San Carlos) to a collection of Mayan stelae (Baluarte de la Solidad); there's even a botanical garden in the Baluarte de Santiago. The **Reducto de San Miguel** to the south of town houses an impressive archaeology museum featuring jade masks recovered from the great Mayan city of Calakmul.

But most impressive is the city itself. Campechanos have renovated the entire old part of the city, restoring it as closely as possible to its colonial appearance. Simply strolling about the place is delightful; another way to see the town is by

Colourfully restored colonial houses in Campeche

Ruins in the jungle at Calakmul

trolley tour, which leaves from the main square almost every hour.

The main attractions outside the city are the ruins of **Edzná**, less than an hour away in the Mérida direction. The ruins of the **Río Bec Route** are farther away and are perfect for the more adventurous traveller, since they are relatively recent excavations and much of the vegetation has been left as it was found. Federal Highway 186, which traverses the Río Bec region, eventually crosses the peninsula to the Caribbean coast at Chetumal. Of the ruins along this route, the most impressive are those of **Calakmul** (classic Mayan architecture in the heart of the jungle near the Guatamala border, with the tallest pyramid in the Yucatán), **Balamkú** (perfectly preserved sculpted walls showing Mayan kings and underworld deities) and **Becán**, surrounded by a dry moat. A trip through the region would take two days and require spending the night at one of the hotels around Chicanná or Xpujil. Several companies offer tours of the region from Campeche.

Chichén Itzá

Chichén Itzá, 120km (75 miles) southeast of Mérida, is the best-preserved and biggest of the Mayan cities. It may have been settled around AD500 by Mayans called 'Itzá' moving north from Guatemala; in Mayan its name means 'mouth of the well of the Itzá'. The city appears to have been abandoned for the first time 125 years after its founding and occupied again in about AD900, after which its most important buildings were constructed. It was to be the last great achievement of Mayan builders. Chichén Itzá was abandoned for good after a war in 1182, though pilgrims continued to visit its sacred *cenote* for centuries. It is possible that Toltec warriors, perhaps led by the legendary Ce Acatl Topiltzín of Tula (Quetzalcóatl), captured Chichén Itzá around the year AD1000. The ruins are in two sections, Chichén Viejo (Old Chichén) and Chichén Nuevo (New Chichén), roughly dating before and after the Toltec conquest.

The Spaniards named the pyramid in Chichén Itzá's new section **El Castillo**. It is in fact a temple to Kukulcán (the serpent god, the Mayan version of Quetzalcóatl) and evidently had importance in Mayan astronomy. There are four flights of stairs with 91 steps on each. Adding the top platform gives 365, the days of the year. The stairs divide nine terraces into 18 on each side, the number of months in the Mayan calendar. At 5pm on the spring and autumn equinoxes, a shadow moves down the right wall of the north staircase like the rippling body of a snake until it reaches the carved serpent head at the base, then moves back up again – Kukulcán descending to earth and returning to

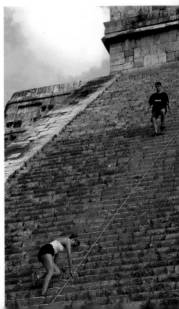

Descending the Kukulcán pyramid at Chichén Itzá

The jade-eyed jaguar inside the Kukulcán pyramid

the heavens. The biannual phenomenon understandably attracts large crowds.

A hot, clammy and crowded climb up a stair-case archaeologists built in-side the pyramid in the 1930s takes you to the plat-form of an earlier temple that holds a red-painted jaguar with jade eyes and mother-of-pearl spots. This is no place for the claustro-phobic. The north chamber of the temple atop the Castillo is decorated with carvings on columns and reliefs of priests in feathered headdresses.

The **Plataforma de Venus**, directly in front of the north staircase, is full of Toltec influence. The faces carved on the sides, with staring eyes and round ear plugs, are not Mayan. You'll find a carving of the Toltec morning star and its sym-bol. a graceful feathered serpent, around the top level, as well as a curious fish with legs (a tadpole perhaps?). Traces of red and green paint are a reminder that this city, too, was once coloured resplendently.

To the east stands the **Templo de los Guerreros** (Temple of the Warriors). The portico of square columns richly carved with warriors in armour fronts steep stairs to the top platform, where a *chac-mool* is centrally placed. These stylised figures are always the same – a reclining man hold-ing a plate on his lap. They may have been stands for burn-ing incense. The temple doorway is formed by snakes whose rattles bend overhead to hold the vanished lintel.

More columns reminiscent of Tula form a portico on the south side of the temple called the **Mercado**, or market. No doubt these colonnades, when roofed, provided relief from the Yucatán sun. The south walls are covered with reliefs of eagles, bears and jaguars. An earlier temple to the *chac-mool* underlies this complex. A rough causeway some 275m (900ft) through the undergrowth leads from the Castillo to the **Cenote Sagrado**. It's a haunting spot, a well 59m (194ft) across, overhung

The Temple of the Warriors is named after its many carved columns

with trees and vines. Here human sacrifices were thrown to propitiate the rain god in times of drought. The legend says the victims were beautiful virgins, but most of the 40-plus skeletons found by dredging were of children. A quantity of offerings in jade and gold have been recovered from the steep-sided well's murky green waters, some 22m (65ft) deep. In 1903 Edward Thompson, the US vice-consul in Mérida, made the first attempt to plunder these riches. He bought the entire site and an adjoining hacienda for $75. Some of his loot has been returned to the museum in Mérida; the rest is in US museums.

To the right of the main area is the **Tzompantli**, a wall of skull reliefs in black and white and decorated with eagles holding human hearts in their talons, all very Toltec in spirit. Next comes the **Templo de los Jaguares** (Temple of the Jaguars), built into the rear wall of the ball court. The reliefs on the lower-level columns describe the creation of the world. Legend has it that tears from the god on the left pillar become waters that give life to plants and animals and then to man. The right pillar is a woman with a skull head representing death. This duality of life and death is a constant theme of religious art in pre-Columbian Mexico. In the centre of the rear wall covered with warriors is a bearded figure who may be Kukulcán.

The doorway of the upper temple is flanked by huge monolithic serpents. Inside are more warriors and fresco fragments of Toltecs fighting with Maya. The **Juego de Pelota** (Ball Court) is the largest in Mexico. The price of defeat, or victory, is vividly described in relief panels at mid-court: a headless captain with serpents streaming like blood from his neck kneels before his opponent, who holds the head and brandishes a knife. Note the protective pads, shoes and costumes of the players.

Old Chichén Itzá is reached by a trail south of the Castillo. All along the way are the mounds of mostly unexcavated structures until you reach one of the city's most unusual buildings, **El Caracol** (The Snail), also called the **Observatory**. Situated in an open space, this round tower has an interior circular stair leading to the rooms where observations may have

been made of Venus and other heavenly bodies. Farther on, the top-heavy one-room **Iglesia** (Church) and **Templo de las Monjas** (Nunnery) are temples heavily adorned in the Puuc style, with the curling Chaac snouts in evidence. The Nunnery was partly blown up by treasure hunters. The **Casa Colorada** (Red House), on a mound and with remains of a classic Mayan roof comb, is

The serpent Kukulcán is ever-present in Chichén Itzá

Inside the Dzitnup *cenote*

one of the oldest at this site, dating from the 7th century.

The southern section of the ruins is a 15-minute walk away, along a small path. Most of the buildings are semi-overgrown. On one, the two Atlantes holding up a door lintel are obvious copies of the warrior pillars at Tula. Other temples and houses are purely Mayan. Ruins in the brush are found in all directions, giving an idea of the vast extent of Chichén Itzá in its prime. A model and explanations in the visitor's centre museum at the entrance are helpful in putting it all in perspective.

All this is a lot to appreciate in one day. If you want to see the ruins thoroughly, plan to stay at one of the several comfortable hotels adjoining the site. The Chichén Itzá ruins are open every day from 8am to 5pm, and there is a sound-and-light show every evening at 8.

Near the ruins is the **Balankanche** cave (open daily 9am–5pm), discovered in 1959 and found to have been used for Mayan rites. It takes a bit of squeezing and stooping to get through to the chambers where offerings to the rain god were made. Jars and an altar have been left as they were found beside a pool where blind fish swim. Tours of the cave can be in either Spanish or English.

Farther east, about 40km (25 miles) in the direction of Cancún, is a lovely *cenote* called **Dzitnup**. You can have a swim here in the clear water illuminated by a sunbeam shining through a hole in the ceiling.

Cancún and Isla Mujeres

Cancún is the point of introduction for the great majority of travellers to Mexico. Aquiline waters, white sand, luxury hotels, a sporting nightlife and even nearby archaeological wonders all serve as lures to the more than two million visitors who come here each year. Cancún may be soulless (at least to anyone looking for adventure and exotic environs), but this region offers the ideal combination of breathtaking natural beauty and the depth of Mexico's long history.

These magnificent Caribbean beaches were the first face of Mexico seen by Europeans, at least as early as 1517. For well over four centuries Quintana Roo, as the Caribbean coast of Yucatán is known, was left to the few rebellious Mayans who could scratch a living in the brush; for everyone else it was a remote place of exile. A small Mayan ruin, **El Rey**, speaks for the fact this was once Maya land – although it was obviously an outpost, not a true settlement.

By now the story is well known: the government's tourism developers, FONA-TUR, fed a 'wish list' into a computer to locate the ideal place for a beach resort. The computer answered 'Can-cún'. The uninhabited 22km (14-mile), hook-shaped is-land had to be developed

White beaches and blue sea bring millions of visitors to Cancún

from scratch, but it had everything nature could provide: an average 243 sunny days a year, a fantastic beach on one side and a tranquil lagoon on the other. As an added touch, Mayan ruins were not far distant.

To construct and service the playground, a new town, Cancún City, was built on the mainland and short causeways connected it to both ends of the island. Only super-deluxe hotels were permitted on Cancún (good cheaper ones have been built in town) and roads and an airport had to be installed. The luxurious complex opened in 1974 and Cancún's fame rapidly spread. Today it is undisputedly Mexico's top resort. It's easy to get around in Cancún: buses and taxis travel between the row of towering hotels that front the beach like a line of dominoes along its one street, Paseo Kukulcán. More than 20,000 rooms in the area offer something for every taste and budget. Most of the dining, shop-

The Hilton Beach Cancún, one of Cancún's largest hotels

ping and entertainment is found at the northern 'hook' of the island, near the **convention centre**.

Sports-minded holiday-makers take to the tennis courts or golf courses, and scuba diving and deep-sea fishing is popular from cruisers and catamarans. But shopping seems to be one of the most popular pastimes in Cancún, with its profusion of grand malls selling everything from designer sunglasses to duty-free jewellery and perfumes. There is a

Traditional baskets being made in the Mercado de Artesanías

more traditional shopping alternative among the handicraft stalls of the **Mercado de Artesanías** on Tulum Boulevard in Cancún City. For some authentic colour, there's a bull-ring in town, with *corridas* year-round on Wednesdays at 4pm. By night, a taste of true Mexico is imported for fiestas at the hotels and the folkloric dinner show at the convention centre. Among the most popular night-time venues, however, are the many clubs and bars. The **Forum by the Sea** houses an impressive collection of nightlife in one seaside entertainment mall.

If you are at all curious to see the real Mexico, leave the beach and glitter long enough to enjoy one of the many interesting excursions. Among the most popular day-trips are to the great Mayan city **Chichén Itzá** (*see page 142*), to the ruins of **Tulum** (*see page 157*), or down the coast to a string of marvellous beaches, some completely untouched, others with bungalows or palm-thatched *palapa* shelters for hammock-slinging and a few with first-class hotels catering for scuba divers. **Punta Bete**, 60km (37 miles) south of Cancún, has good swimming off a picture-postcard beach with coco palms. **Akumal**, 104km (65 miles) from Cancún, is famed for diving. There's even an underwater museum where you can swim among cannon and other artifacts found by divers. **Xcacel** (pronounced *sha-SELL*), 120km (72 miles) south of Cancún, is another very attractive and uncrowded swimming beach.

Although only 10km (6 miles) from Cancún, **Isla Mujeres** is quite another world. This 'Island of Women' was named as such for the numerous Mayan fertility idols found by Cortés when he arrived here in 1519. Today it is favoured by those who appreciate the convenience of flying into Cancún, but prefer a more easy-going, laid-back pace. The beaches are exquisite, the snorkelling and diving are excellent and there is an ample selection of casual, beachfront restaurants. Accommodation ranges from budget-beach style rooms to super-luxury guesthouses, with the common

Marine Theme Parks

Where underground rivers meet the sea on the Yucatán coast, the mixture of fresh and sea water attracts a wide range of aquatic life. **Xcaret**, 72km (50 miles) south of Cancún, is an 'eco-archeological' theme park where you can snorkel through an underground river system, swim with dolphins and enjoy a night of Mexican music. Farther south, **Akumal**, the 'Place of the Turtles', is famous for its snorkelling and diving, as is the beautiful but extremely overcrowded **Xel-Há** lagoon, a large natural aquarium full of iridescent tropical fish. They all have restaurants, shops, changing rooms and organised activities, and all are attractive sites, but you'll leave thinking how beautiful they must have been before the tour buses came.

Laid-back Isla Mujeres is far from the frenzy of Cancún

denominator being travellers who have an appreciation for tranquillity. Ferries from Puerto Juárez just north of Cancún or Punta Sam (cars carried) take passengers over to the island for an enjoyable day of exploring or for longer stays. Swimmers head for **Playa del Norte**, snorkellers for **El Garrafón**'s coral reef. A curiosity for expert divers are the underwater caves where 'sleeping' sharks lie on the bottom. The island is only 2km (1½ miles) wide and 8km (5 miles) long, with the concentration of hotels, shops and seafood restaurants at the northern end.

Cozumel

The island of Cozumel, 20km (12 miles) off the Yucatán and roughly 50km long and 15km wide (30 by 9 miles), lies near the northern end of a barrier reef of coral that is second only to Australia's Great Barrier Reef. The coral reef produces white sand and prevents waves from roiling the bottom and the result is crystal-clear, light aquamarine water that is pleasantly warm but not tepid. In other words, these waters are absolute heaven for swimmers, snorkellers, divers and even passengers in a glass-bottomed boat.

A proficiency card is required for scuba diving, but instructors will deliver one after alarmingly few hours and will act as guides on reefs of varying complexity. Palancar Reef is 5km (3 miles) long and drops sharply into a trough 1,620m deep (5,350ft) with 75m (250ft) visibility. San Francisco Reef, about 545m (500yds) long and 15m (50ft) deep is easier, and Yacab, 9m (30ft) deep, is more suitable for beginners.

Boats to the reefs and **Parque Chancanab** pick up passengers at hotel docks and provide refreshments and gear. The underwater population is gaudy: delicate blue angel fish, black-and-white striped sergeant majors, red squirrel

The coral reefs off Cozumel are a delight for scuba divers

fish with big eyes and spiny backs, intense, electric-coloured schools of tiny wrasse dazzling like a cloud of sparks, butterfly fish with a round black spot, yellow and silvery grunts and rainbow-hued parrot fish are just a few of the common varieties you can encounter close to the shore. Farther out you might see a ray flap by like a giant bird. The marine park at Chancanab is a good place to learn to identify some of the count-

Relaxing in San Miguel

less varieties – and to get quite close enough to a moray eel.

With so much to see in a calm sea, fewer people swim in the hotel pools. Poolside is great for sunning, socialising and snacking. Beachside, there's tennis, windsurfing, parasailing, chasing about on the noisy waverunners and sailing, as well as cycling. Near mid-point amid the beaches along the western side of the island, iguanas scuttle in the modest Mayan ruins at **San Gervasio**. Turtles come ashore in July to lay eggs near Punta Molas.

San Miguel is basically a giant shopping mall interspersed with a few lively restaurants and bars, where margaritas are served in goblets the size of goldfish bowls. The din of rock music from radios is constant and heavy traffic gets noisy along the seafront Malecón. Hotels offer evening entertainment but, though there are clubs in town, Cozumel isn't really big on nightlife. It's fun to join the crowd at outdoor tables around the zócalo and walk back to your hotel escorted by fireflies. In winter, cruise ships

Enticing shades of blue near Tulum

unload up to 2,000 passengers a day in an assault on the shops of San Miguel, where most Mexican handicrafts and some designer clothes are found. Ever-eager shop owners put up permanent signs reading 'Welcome passengers of the...' and hang up a new ship's name every day. Prices are quoted in dollars, which are practically the second coin of this realm. To get away from it all, as you may well be tempted to do, board one of the charter boats that go out game-fishing from the harbour.

A ferry connects with buses on the mainland at **Playa del Carmen**, a very popular beach spot for those who are interested less in snorkelling and diving and more in having a good beach holiday with lovely water, quirky surroundings, good restaurants and fun nightlife. It's about 45 minutes away by ferry from Cozumel. The town also has a central location, perfect for getting to nearby ruins or to other spots up and down the coast.

Tulum and the Lower Caribbean Coast

By Mayan standards **Tulum** was a small trading city, built around 1200 when Mayan architecture had become decadent. It was undoubtedly a port, and may also have served as a fortress protecting sea trade routes. It was discovered by the explorer Juan de Grijalva, who navigated along the east coast of the Yucatán in 1518. Until it was conquered by the Spanish in 1530, Tulum was a prosperous town. It was surrounded by a wall with five gates, and probably had to be defended during the wars that contributed to the decline of the Mayas in Yucatán.

Tulum's glory is its setting. The **Castillo**, the central temple on a high platform, commands an incomparable view over the sea and coast. Perfect little beaches spread out below. The site is open daily 8am–7pm in summer and 7am–6pm in winter. The **Templo de los Frescos** (Temple of the Frescoes), in the centre of the compound, has faded paintings inside and out of offerings to the god Yumkin and of fish and fertility figures. A stucco relief of the god holding a snake fills a niche by the door. Notice how the cornice angles form faces. Yumkin is seen again over the entrance to his own temple to the left of the Castillo.

Of special interest is a stretch of ancient Mayan road that divides the compound. Though they didn't have wheeled vehicles, the Mayans did build paved roads, called *sacbeob*, perhaps for use in ceremonial processions.

More of these roads may be seen at **Cobá**, a very interesting 8th-century Mayan

Yumkin, the deity worshipped in Tulum, is the 'Descending God', always shown diving head-first. It is thought that he represented the setting sun. Central to Mayan religion was the fear that the sun might never return from his nightly journey into the underworld.

site on lakes some 40km (25 miles) inland. A network of *sacbeob* crosses Cobá's mostly unexcavated ruins, which extend into the jungle. Cobá was evidently a very large city, probably founded by Mayans from Guatemala, for the very steep pyramids here are similar to the ones at Tikal. At Cobá you can share the archaeologist's feelings of discovery as you follow jungle trails surrounded by mysterious mounds. Bring insect repellent and wear walking shoes.

The beaches along this part of the coast are lonely and pristine. Just south of Tulum is the **Punta Allen peninsula**, which is a perfect place to get away from the crowded beaches to the north. At the very tip is the fishing village of Punta Allen.

Tulum's watchtower on the coast may have served as a lighthouse

The peninsula shelters a lagoon that is part of a large biosphere reserve called **Sian Ka'an**; much of the coast here is mangrove, and inland it gives way to tropical forest and savanna, with abundant wildlife including jaguars, howler monkeys, manatees and endangered turtles. It is possible to take boat tours of the lagoon, and out to the reef where the snorkelling is excellent.

Farther south on Highway 307 you will see a turn-off for the **Majahual peninsula**, a favourite place for divers who come to explore the **Chinchorro reef**. When you've reached this point, you will have left civilisation pretty far behind you. If you remain on 307, you will come to **Laguna Bacalar**, a freshwater lake 100km (60 miles) long that is as clear and blue as the Caribbean because it is fed by *cenotes*.

Finally you arrive at the end of the line, the state capital, **Chetumal**. This city has one good thing going for it: the wonderful **Museo de la Cultura Maya** (Museum of Mayan Culture, open Tues–Thur 9am–7pm, Fri–Sun 9am–8pm) with all kinds of interactive exhibits that explain some of the Maya's cosmology, astronomy, calendrics and society. It is a modern, beautifully laid-out museum. From Chetumal you can go either to Belize or inland and follow the Río Bec Route (*see page 142*).

OAXACA AND CHIAPAS

Visits to this region of beautiful highlands, endless beaches and impressive jungles are never long enough. The colonial jewels of Oaxaca and San Cristóbal, with their large Indian populations, are fascinating places for simply watching and listening. When the urge to do something more active strikes, there are many ruins, Indian villages and solitary vistas to seek out. Or perhaps you simply want to relax by the ocean and enjoy some Oaxacan beach culture.

Oaxaca

Oaxaca (pronounced *Wa-ha-ka*) is the state that seems to have everything – beaches, highlands, handicrafts, ruins and increasingly easy air access to the state's capital and beach resorts. But if you fly directly in and out of the resorts without paying a visit to Oaxaca City, you will have missed one of the most charming colonial cities in Mexico.

➤ **Oaxaca City** will slow down your clock. The pressure is off the minute you settle into a chair at one of the cafés bordering the central gathering place, the **zócalo**. Enjoy a *café con leche* or a *cerveza* and have your shoes shined while you watch the world go by. Streets around the plaza and the adjoining Alameda are open to pedestrians only. A balloon-seller ambles past, children playing tag will dart and squeal around the fountains, an Indian woman with her hair carefully braided will hold up for your appraisal a belt she has woven and the rich aroma of

> Mezcal is a speciality of Oaxaca and certain areas of central Mexico. It is distilled in a similar way to tequila, but uses the juice of different agave plants. Mezcal has a stronger taste and smell. In Oaxaca, it is bottled with a maguey worm (*gusano*) preserved in the alcohol.

sizzling food from a pavement stall floats by.

As afternoon turns into
evening, the bandstand
lights up, dimly, and the municipal band serenades the
strollers who come just to
while away a little time in
such lovely surroundings
with marimba music or old-
fashioned waltzes. Soon it's
time to head for a restaurant
and enjoy some of the food
for which Oaxaca is famous.

There are no big modern
buildings in Oaxaca. Most of
the downtown area was built
in colonial times with the
lovely green stone for which
the city is famous. All buildings tend to be low and

Santo Domingo in Oaxaca

broad with thick walls – an architectural style that was born
from several serious earthquakes that struck the city during
the colonial era. Even the churches' bell towers are low and
squat, as is the case of the **cathedral**, which has been reconstructed a couple of times. The façade presents the viewer
with all the elements of the highly stylised Oaxacan baroque
with its heavy and elaborate framing of the main panels, the
wave-like depiction of clouds and the detailed depiction of its
principal scene, the assumption of the Virgin. The overall
effect is one of solidity and stateliness.

Indeed, many of the loveliest buildings in Oaxaca are
churches and convents. The most beautiful is **Santo Domingo**, set back on a plaza six blocks north of the zócalo. The

church and convent were begun in 1575 and rebuilt with walls 2m (6ft) thick after being destroyed by an earthquake. More destruction resulted from the Wars of La Reforma in the second half of the 19th century, when Santo Domingo and its monastery were used as a barracks and stable. In 1898, the church was beautifully restored under the guidance of Bishop Gillow.

The barrel vault and walls are encrusted with ornamental gilt stucco and paintings, made more dazzling by a white plaster background and black outlining. St Dominic stands in the centre of the golden three-tiered main altar screen. The sumptuous **Capilla del Rosario** (Rosary Chapel) to the right attracts the most devotees. The ceiling just inside the entrance is covered by a many-branched genealogical tree, with moustachioed grandees and queenly dames representing the ancestry of St Dominic. It culminates not in the saint, but in a Virgin and child, added during restoration. A magical moment may envelop the church when an Indian woman, kneeling in a shaft of light from the stained glass windows, spontaneously lifts her voice in a hymn.

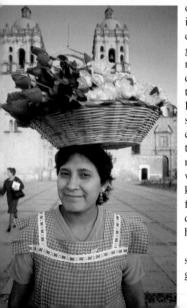

Roses for sale on the square in front of Santo Domingo

The monastery next door stayed in the hands of the government, which recently performed an impressive restoration to the entire building and surrounding grounds. It now houses an ambitious museum, the **Museo Regional de Oaxaca** (open Tues–Sun 10am–8pm), which presents in several galleries the story of the region from the arrival of the first inhabitants, to the first large civilisations, to the conquering Spaniards, to the long colonial period, to Independence and all the way to the present. There is also an ethnology exhibition on the

The golden altar screen inside Santo Domingo church

present Indian population of the surrounding valleys. A lot can be learned here that will be helpful when visiting the villages and ruins that lie in the surrounding area.

Clearly, the centrepiece of the museum's collection is the Mixtec treasures found in Tomb 7 in Monte Albán. More than 500 pieces of jewellery and artifacts were discovered in this tomb in 1932. Here is the famous gold burial mask and breastplate, a necklace of gold turtles, huge pearls, jewellery of coral, amber and jade, cups of rock crystal and a skull partly covered in turquoise mosaic. Other skulls show traces of brain operations – but no indication whether the patients survived.

The Mixtecs mastered the art of crafting gold by the 'lost wax' method. The form was first carved in clay, then covered with wax and overlaid again by clay. The wax was melted and drained and the cavity filled with molten gold. Then the clay was removed and the gold image polished to perfection.

In another room you'll find some of the glass beads the conquistadors traded to the Indians for gold. If they had found Tomb 7, they would have melted the treasure into ingots, as they did with most Indian gold.

Another marvellous collection is in the **Museo Rufino Tamayo** on Calle Morelos (open Mon, Wed–Sat 10am–2pm and 4–7pm, Sun 10am–3pm). Tamayo, a Oaxaca painter who died in his 90s in 1991, converted a colonial house and patio and filled it with his superb selection of ancient Mexican art from every period and civilisation. Among the many masterpieces, look for the charming little Olmec 'sunbathers' in room 1; the clay model of a ball game with spectators and a great helmeted Nayarit warrior in room 2; and two amazing terracotta figures in room 3: an old man 'chewing herbs' and an enthroned figure of the skeletal God of Death.

The **Basílica de la Soledad**, two blocks farther east (open daily 7am–2pm and 4–9pm), honours the city's patron saint, whose image appeared miraculously at this spot in a box on the back of a mysterious *burro*. This Virgin is extremely popular throughout the state. There's a fun little museum behind the church to the left that exhibits in random order all kinds of memorabilia and honour paid to the Virgin (open Mon–Sat 10am–2pm and 4–6pm, Sun 11am–2pm). In the plaza in front you will find several ice-cream vendors (it's a sort of tradition to eat ice-cream after visiting the basílica). Also for sale are religious curios, including little *milagros* – small tin images of legs, arms, hearts or animals that the faithful buy to pin up in the chapel of their favourite saint as a form of petition.

Oaxaca has a large festival every July called the **Guelaguetza**, which showcases the costumes and dances of the many Indian villages in the state. It is a popular festival that fills the city for two weeks. On the last two Mondays of the month there are performances of the region's dances in the large outdoor amphitheatre on the Cerro del Fortín hill. On preceding Sunday nights, university students dance the *Bani Stui Gulal* in the plaza in front of La Soledad; this is the history of the region presented through dance.

The markets of Oaxaca and neighbouring villages would be sufficient reason for your visit. Oaxaca is particularly famous for its weavings (especially those coloured with cochineal and other natural dyes), black pottery and *alebrijes*, which are wood carvings of fantastical animals. For other items, Indian *tianguis* (street markets) are all over town and women and children offer their wares wherever you turn. Unusually fine handicraft shops occupy the interiors and patios of colonial mansions. Look for most of them on the pedestrians-only Alcalá and Cinco de Mayo, streets that run north from the plaza to Santo Domingo.

But there's also action every day in the covered **Mercado**

Fresh fruit and vegetables in the Mercado de Abastos

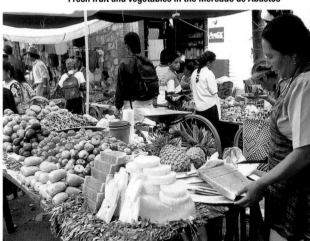

Benito Juárez behind the zócalo, and on Saturdays in the sprawling **Mercado de Abastos** west of the Periférico loop. Both are places where the populace comes for supplies. Each section has its own cloud of scents: sweet, fermented, spicy, floral, fishy and so on. And each has stalls heaped with the freshest, most colourful produce. You'll find straw hats and baskets, embroidered blouses, rugs, shawls and sandals in the covered market. The quality may not be as high as

Markets in the Valley Villages

Each village in the valley of Oaxaca has its own market day, and each its special product. The Sunday market in Tlacolula is one of the best. On the way, stop at the Tule Tree, an ancient ahuehuete cypress, an incredible 60m (164ft) in circumference. A short detour to Teotitlán del Valle brings you to the valley's most famous weaving centre. Along the road you'll see fields of *maguey*, the spiked leaf agave grown here to make mezcal, the local tequila. You can visit a distillery to see it done and to sample the product. Tlacolula merchants will show you how to drink it straight, with a special reddish salt that has powdered *maguey* worms in it. Some bottles come with a *gusano* (worm) inside to prove it's the real thing.

The Friday market in Ocotlán is not very touristy, and the Thursday market in Zaachila even less so, but they couldn't be more picturesque. The market women don't particularly like having cameras or camcorders stuck in their faces, so be respectful and ask before you shoot. See the many varieties of fresh and dried chile peppers, watch how each fruit is polished and piled artistically, notice how the mangoes are carved like pine cones. You'll see women wearing the same shawls, blouses and red-and-white skirts that are sold in Oaxaca's craft shops. San Bartolo Coyotepec, on the road to Ocotlán, is the source of velvety black pottery. Stop at any of the houses with pots outside to see them being made.

in the craft shops, but they're authentic; Oaxacans buy them too. Bargaining is part of every transaction.

Early on Saturday, Indians from the surrounding countryside come into the Mercado de Abastos with chickens and pigs, hand-made brooms and sacks of charcoal to sell. When they've done their business, they fill up with enchiladas wrapped in banana leaves at the numerous food counters nearby.

A potter at work in Oaxaca

Another place to try, particularly if you're looking for apparel or weavings, is the **Mercado Artesanías** at the corner of JP García and Zaragoza.

Mitla

Trips to the markets can be combined with visits to some of Mexico's most interesting ruins and attractions. The road to Tlacolula continues on to **Yagul**, 35km (21 miles) east of Oaxaca and Mitla. Most tours sail right past Yagul, but the pleasure of exploring this city of Zapotec and Mixtec influence is well worth the short detour. From the crumbled fortress with its cactus sentinels, you look down on a roofless labyrinth of a palace, a ball court and the full sweep of the valley. Perhaps because it has only been partly excavated and is usually empty of visitors, Yagul can seem to be your own discovery. The site is open daily 8am–5.30pm.

Mitla comes next, about 40km (25 miles) east of Oaxaca. The ruins are right in the village (open daily 8am–5pm). These palaces and courtyards of 15th-century Mixtec design

Mitla's 15th-century Mixtec palaces are wonderfully preserved

were inhabited at the time of the Conquest and most were used, rather than destroyed, by the Spaniards, which explains their excellent state of preservation. The exception was the temple, as usual now covered by a church.

The palaces are unlike anything you'll see elsewhere. They are covered by panels of projecting mosaic composed of little limestone bricks tightly fitted without cement. The concept is unique and the work that went into it immense. Because some of the designs resemble the scrollwork of Greek friezes, they are called *grecas*. The massive stone lintels and pillars were somehow dragged from a quarry 20km (13 miles) away.

Across the road, the **church group** of three patios shows that the mosaics were originally painted white on a red background. Mitla is a Zapotec town today and the local guides will claim the palace-builders were of their ethnic group. Who can blame them? In the town, the **Museo de Arte**

Zapoteca (formerly known as the Museo Frisell, open daily 9am–5pm), exhibits Zapotec figurines found in the valley by American archaeologists based here.

Monte Albán

Monte Albán, on a high ridge 8km (5 miles) west of Oaxaca, is an astonishing sacred Zapotec city that for more than 1,200 years embodied the grandeur of one of ancient Mexico's most important civilisations. The site itself (open daily 9am–6pm) is quite extraordinary, a mountain falling off steeply on all sides into valleys. Around 500BC the mountain crest was levelled by enormous effort to create a ceremonial plaza 300m long and 200m wide (980 by 650ft) for temples, a *juego de pelota* (ball court), an observatory and palaces for the priest-rulers. In AD700 all this was abandoned, though the surrounding hillside was later used as a burial ground (where the Mixtec treasures of Tomb 7 and other finds have been unearthed). Apparently the ancient city was closed to all but priests and nobles. The remains of the houses and terraced fields of the peasantry who supported them covered the mountain, where many unexcavated mounds are visible.

Lifted into the open sky, Monte Albán seems designed as a meeting place of men and gods. One can easily imagine how dazzling the plaza must have been when its monumental structures were covered with plaster and painted red and white. The pyramidal platforms originally held temples and palaces of wood. If you're on a tour or engage a guide, you'll probably begin by circling the ruins from behind in order to visit **Tomb 104**. Burials were usually beneath the floors of houses. Descending steps into this one, you need a torch to see the head of a rain god and some faded frescoes over the entrance to the crypt. Then a path through the underbrush emerges on to the **north platform**, overlooking a sunken

Monte Albán's famous 'dancers' remain an enigma

patio and the whole complex. To the right, a massive platform covers an earlier building. Again a torch is needed to enter a narrow passage and see the original carved façade inside.

The next structure shelters the **Danzantes**, slabs carved soon after 500BC showing naked men and women in gesturing poses that earned them the name of 'dancers'. They have puzzled archaeologists for years. Some appear to be swimming, others are deformed, or are apparently cut open to expose their organs. Some have beards or negroid features alien to the Zapotecs, but similar to some Olmec faces. They may represent prisoners of war, or perhaps sacrifical victims. Another theory is that they are a kind of medical textbook, illustrating illnesses and surgical operations.

The arrow-shaped structure at this end of the plaza (Building J) is angled eastward and has a star symbol on its base, giving rise to the idea that it was aligned to serve as an observatory. Carvings of upside-down (ie defeated) men and hieroglyphic symbols on the walls, however, support the argument that it was a monument to military conquests. Monte Albán writing is different from the glyphs of the Olmecs and Mayas and has not been completely deciphered.

The view from the top of the partly excavated **south platform** is superb, taking in the three mountain ranges converging on Oaxaca. The eastern line of buildings is called **El Palacio**, for it may have been a palatial residence. In the centre of the plaza are the remains of a temple and its staircase. Leaving the complex, on the right is a small **ball court**. The stone 'seats' on one side seem too narrow for spectators. Were they part of the game? This is another of many Mexican mysteries.

There's a museum (open daily 9am–6pm) exhibiting carvings and models that help explain Monte Albán's successive phases and its relations with the contemporary cultures of Teotihuacán and the Mayas. Some 500 years after the city's unexplained abandonment, the Mixtec tribe moved into the valley and ruled over the Zapotecs. They used Monte Albán as a cemetery, sometimes appropriating Zapotec graves. When the Aztecs dominated Mexico, the Mixtecs retreated to the hills, where they live today, while the Zapotecs stayed on in the valley. Mini-buses from Oaxaca run direct to Monte Albán from the Hotel Mesón del Ángel at Calle Mina 518.

Monte Albán stands on an artificially levelled mountaintop

The Oaxacan Coast

The Pacific Coast that borders Oaxaca state has become known as the area to travel in Mexico if you are looking for a pristine, wild, unspoiled stretch of beach. The first town to gain recognition was **Puerto Escondido**, considered one of the world's top surf sites. Its renowned **Playa Zicatela** is nicknamed 'the Mexican Pipeline', and is the site of an annual competition during the autumn swells. Throughout the year, the town attracts a young and very hip international crowd, with its laid-back village ambience, attractive and good-value accommodation and nearby nature excursions. At the centre of town is a curving beach where fishermen land their boats and sell their catch on the spot.

One street back is the *Adoquín*, a pedestrianised stretch of street named after the hexagonal-shaped, interlocking bricks

The Only Way to Go

Wherever there's a road in Mexico, there's a bus. The bus is the country's favourite mode of travel – very cheap, comfortable, and a good way to see the scenery and enjoy the people. First-class buses are usually first class, with air-conditioning and a bathroom; second class can be okay, but are often uncomfortably crowded. The two services usually operate from different stations. Head for the Central de Autobuses (or Camiones) de Primera Clase.

Directo doesn't always live up to its name. Especially on the outskirts of town, the bus driver will often stop to let people on or off. A lot of eating goes on during long bus rides. You may be offered a snack or a drink, and your neighbour will be pleased at your offer to share your own provisions. It's a good way to break the ice and strike up a conversation. Many drivers hang a motto over their seat. A favourite that may give you second thoughts: 'If this is my last trip, God, may it lead to you.' Not to worry – bus travel in Mexico is quite safe.

used in its paving. Hotels, shops, restaurants, bars, travel agencies and other services are all conveniently located here. Though small, the town enjoys an active and varied nightlife, with a strong live music scene during winter months. From dining to hotels, Puerto, as it is called locally, offers one of the best overall beach venues in Mexico.

A few hours by boat or down the coast road from Puerto Escondido is the even more laid-back **Puerto Ángel**. This place truly is a 'sleepy little fishing village'. You'll eat lobster or fish on the beach under a thatched *palapa* shelter and

A laid-back beach restaurant in Puerto Escondido

snooze in a hammock strung between two palms. Turtles come ashore to lay their eggs in this area and one of the country's top turtle preservation facilities lies between Puerto Escondido and Puerto Ángel, in the constant struggle to protect this endangered species against poachers.

A few spots, such as several of the inlets along **Bahías de Huatulco**, are officially slated for development by FONATUR, the government agency that created Cancún and Ixtapa. Located 40km (25 miles) to the south of Puerto Ángel, it has 36 beaches on a spectacular coastline spread across nine bays. The fact that the area has been slow to catch on has resulted in a curious mix of ultra-modern infrastructure, few distractions and unspoiled natural areas. Huatulco has what it takes to attract visitors – golf, tennis, water sports, fishing, a few restaurants and night spots, luxury accommodation and direct flights from selected US cities – but hasn't developed its own distinct personality yet. For now, Huatulco is ideal for those who want to enjoy the beauty of nature during the day, then retreat to the well-appointed comfort of a luxury hotel by night.

Palenque

In 1840, the intrepid American explorer John Lloyd Stephens and his artist-companion Frederick Catherwood came down from the Guatemala Highlands into the Mexican state of Chiapas, drawn by rumours of a Maya city in ruins. Near the village of Santo Domingo they were led by Indians into the jungle and soon, to their elation, they were surrounded by massive stones. Stephens wrote: 'Through an opening in the trees we saw the front of a large building richly ornamented with stuccoed figures on the pilasters, curious and elegant, with trees growing close against it, their branches entering the doors; in style and effect it was unique, extraordinary and mournfully beautiful…'

Palenque's Palace tower

The ruins of **Palenque** are still mournfully beautiful, especially when emerging from eddies of mist in early morning (the site is open daily 8am–4.45pm). Though major buildings have now been cleared, the grassy clearing closely hemmed in by low hills and dense rainforest contains only a fraction of the 500-

odd structures identified so far at this massive site. Walk a few steps along forest paths and you will find yourself back in the jungle that still engulfs most of the city. Stephens recognised what sets Palenque apart from such overpowering monumental sites as Chichén Itzá. At Palenque, the workmanship is far more artistic and harmonious, less

Palenque

0   200 m

0   200 yds

designed to inspire awe and with a more practical bent. There are niches with platforms for sleeping and a steam bath; a pagoda-style tower, with its large windows commanding a sweeping view of the plain and forest, may have been a watchtower and has no counterpart in Maya architecture.

Palenque's prime spanned AD500 to 900, the height of the Maya classic period. Nah-Chan (the Maya name, meaning 'house of the serpent') was a city-state ruled by priest-kings, the greatest of whom were Pacal and his sons, Chan-Bahlum and Xan-Kul, who ruled from roughly 615 to 720. The last dated inscription in Palenque is 799 and some time after that the city was invaded from the north. It appears to have been largely abandoned in the 9th century.

The **Templo de las Inscripciones** is an eight-tiered pyramid with 69 steps leading to a temple whose inscriptions are hieroglyphics, giving Pacal's pedigree. Chan-Bahlum is also represented on the pillars. This pyramid, handsome enough in itself, turned out to be unique – in 1952, the government archaeologist, Alberto Ruz l'Huillier, lifted one of the unusual paving stones of the temple and discovered a rubble-filled staircase. After four seasons of digging out stone and mortar to a depth of 21m (70ft), Ruz came to a chamber where a stone box held some jade ornaments and a pearl. Battering through a wall 4m (12ft) thick, the workers found another room and in it a casket containing the skeletons of six young men, evidently sacrificed to guard a tomb. But where was the tomb?

A huge triangular stone blocked one wall. Digging around it, Ruz broke into a third chamber, where he saw 'a huge magic grotto… delicate festoons of stalactites hung like tassels of a curtain, and the stalagmites on the floor looked like the drippings of a great candle… Across the walls marched stucco figures in low relief.' In the centre of the vaulted room, 10m (33ft) long and now opened for the first time in more than a thousand years, was a large slab carved with a jewel-

The Mayan ruins of Palenque, a huge site surrounded by forest

draped figure wearing a feathered crown. The excited archaeologists brought jacks to lift the heavy slab. Beneath another stone lid, in a narrow sarcophagus, lay the skeleton of Lord Pacal, his face covered with a mask of jade mosaic. The body was surrounded by jade ornaments and adorned with a collar, rings and ear ornaments of jade. In a scene reminiscent of the opening of Tutankhamen's tomb in Egypt, Ruz had discovered the only known Maya pyramid built for a royal burial. A strange mortared duct leads from the tomb to the top of the stairs. It is believed to have been a way for Pacal's spirit to speak to the living world. The large, heavy slab must have been placed here before the pyramid itself was finished, so the entire structure was probably built while Lord Pacal was still alive and made ready for his burial.

Until recently it was possible for visitors to climb the pyramid and to descend the stairs into the crypt. However, increasing numbers put too much stress on the building, and the condensation from their breath created problems with mildew, so it has had to be closed. The ornaments found here are now in the Museo Nacional de Antropología in Mexico City, in a reconstruction of the tomb. A stone in the grass before the pyramid marks the grave of Alberto Ruz, facing the tomb he discovered.

A small stream that the Mayas paved over separates El Palacio from an amphitheatre formed at the jungle's edge by the mounds of four beautiful 7th-century temples erected by Chan-Bahlum. The largest, on the left, is the **Templo de la Cruz** (Temple of the Cross), so called because of the cross-shaped tree of life design. To the right is a relief panel of a

The Templo de las Inscripciones contained a unique royal tomb

God of the Dead in a jaguar cloak, smoking a cigar; to the right is Chan-Bahlum in leggings and a quetzal feather headdress. The crests of these temples are called 'roof combs'. The mansard slope of the roofs peculiar to Palenque is reflected in thatched roofs still used today. The **Templo de la Cruz Foliada** (Temple of the Foliated Cross) straight ahead has key-hole arches and a panel with a leafy tree of life. The roof comb of the facing **Templo del Sol** (Temple of the Sun) is well preserved and so are the heavy stucco external friezes. Inside, Chan-Bahlum faces an underworld god against a heraldic device of shields and lances. The word in Maya for shield is Pacal, the dynasty's name. The small temple is called Templo XIV – here we find the ruler dancing before a kneeling female figure, presenting an offering.

Beyond the Palacio, the outlines of the ball court are visible; farther on are five temples called the **Grupo del Norte** (Northern Group), whose purpose is not known. To the left of this group is the **Templo del Conde**. A picaresque character named Baron Waldeck lived in its ruins in 1832. Waldeck was employed by the Irish Lord Kingsborough to help prove the theory that the Mayas were the Lost Tribes of Israel. Kingsborough refused to believe that such a civilisation could have been created without influence from elsewhere. He rode his hobby horse into bankruptcy and died in a debtors' prison.

A small **museum** (open daily 9am–1pm and 2–5pm) in the trees past the Grupo del Norte must be visited, if only to see the superb terracotta portrait head of a Maya noble-priest. There is a fine panel of the coronation of Xan-Kul, who followed Chan-Bahlum. One of the figures holding his throne is moustachioed and since Mayas, like most Indians, do not grow facial hair, the presence of bearded faces is always intriguing. Photographs show how the tomb of Lord Pacal looked when it was found.

Colectivos (minibuses) run to and from the ruins and town. Lacandón Indians sell bows and arrows under the trees by a refreshment stand. There is a small airport at Palenque but the main airport serving the area is at Villahermosa on the Gulf coast, some two hours away by road. The town of Palenque

The slash-and-burn farming technique practised by the peasants of Chiapas results in heavy soil erosion and landslides that wash out sections of road every rainy summer. This area contains no temples dedicated to the god of rain – it had no need of his assistance.

The sparkling waters of Agua Azul

has little of interest to the tourist, but there are hotels, a few with pools. For further excursions, a guide can lead you on horseback along trails to unexcavated ruins looming in the forest. Small planes from Palenque and Villahermosa can be chartered to visit the important Maya cities of Bonampak, with its famous frescoes, and Yaxchilán; both can also be visited on fairly arduous road safaris arranged through the hotels.

The bus from Palenque to San Cristóbal de las Casas takes nearly five hours to cover 207km (128 miles) through the gorgeous foothills and Sierra Madre de Chiapas mountains of the southernmost Mexican state, Chiapas. Along the road, women sell bags of oranges and tacos. Some 58km (36 miles) out of Palenque, the turn-off to **Agua Azul** (Blue Water) leads after 5km (3 miles) to a nature reserve protecting a staircase of pools with water as blue as the sky. The river spills over projecting limestone platforms, each producing a low, foaming waterfall and a blue basin. The ledges and pools step down the hillside through green forest, an enchanting and unexpected refuge.

After Ocosingo, as the road climbs, you'll pass ragged coffee plantations where women and children rake beans to dry on the ground. The ferns, elephant-ear plants and tall hardwood trees of the jungle give way to pine forests where wild lantana and dahlias brighten the hillsides. In these parts, nearly every male over the age of 12 seems to carry a machete and wear a straw hat. Mud and thatch huts look very much like the temples on the pyramids in Palenque.

San Cristóbal de las Casas

The charm of **San Cristóbal de las Casas** is its untouristy, strongly Indian flavour. Two Maya tribes predominate in the surrounding villages: the Tzotzils and the Tzeltals, with a few shy Lacandones turning up from the forest on market days. Each village has some identifying trademark in its costumes, but all the men wear knee-length white shorts. The Tzotzil-speaking men of Zinancantán wear hot pink tunics and flat hats trailing ribbons. The women wear blue wraparound skirts and distinctive white *huipiles* embroidered with an ancient, intricate Mayan rectangular pattern in red. The men wear sandals, but most women go barefoot and many carry babies in hammock-like *rebozos* slung over their backs. Their hands are always busy, weaving a coloured belt or making a doll. When seated in the sun, they fold their *rebozos* like bath towels and place them on their heads.

A Mayan Indian of Zinancantán in distinctive headgear

The town is old Spanish, though without the flamboyance of the colonial cities of central Mexico, and its history is sombre. The region was invaded in 1527 by a particularly cruel conquistador, Diego de Mazariegos, whom Cortés had sent on a punitive expedition because the local tribes were behind in their tribute payments.

Mazariegos founded the town and called it La Villa Real de Chiapas. He captured Indians, branded them and sold them as slaves. This brought him into conflict with Bartolomé de las Casas, a Dominican friar who had sailed with Columbus and had become a staunch protector of the Indians. Las Casas, whose name the town now bears, became bishop of Chiapas in 1545. (You saw him in Diego Rivera's mural in the Palacio Nacional in Mexico City, shaking his cross at the conquistador.) The region had no wealth to attract settlers, and such administration as there was came from Guatemala. Chiapas did not become fully a part of Mexico until after independence in the 19th century.

The houses of San Cristóbal de las Casas have red tile roofs, walls of faded pastel colours and iron grilles over the windows. The pavements are high; there are big gutters and rainpipes jutting out over the street for the heavy rains. A big doorway usually opens on to an inner patio where family life goes on in full view. Hotels use this arrangement to create flowery courtyards where guests can read in the sun and sip their drinks. One of these hostelries was the home of Mazariegos. It can get cold at this altitude (2,262m/ 7,465ft) and many hotel rooms have fireplaces.

Traditional weaving in San Cristóbal's large market

The Avenida General Utrilla will lead gently upwards to the **Santo Domingo** church, a 16th- and 17th-century baroque beauty of buff stone with leafy encrustations on its twisting columns. A quiet gathering of Indian women and their children sit under trees beside the church, weaving and selling their wares. The **Museo de los Altos de Chiapas** adjoining the church (open Tues–Sun 10am–4pm) houses a rich exhibition of the textiles and embroidery patterns of Chiapas villages. Present-day examples of these same crafts are sold across the street at **Sna Jolobil** (Tzotzil for 'house of weaving'), a cooperative representing the women of 20 villages dedicated to preserving traditional handwork. Along this street are shops selling men's belts of braided leather, fancy machetes, baskets made from armadillo armour, embroidered bags, *sarapes* (ponchos) and wool rugs.

Santo Domingo's ornate façade

At the top of the rise, the *mercado* spreads out for many blocks in the open air around a market building. It is a refreshingly authentic scene, vivid with the costumes of the surrounding villages, the scents and colours of their produce, the squeals and squawks of their animals and the sing-song sibilance of Tzotzil.

Tourists are warned quite seriously not to photograph these Indians without their permission. Good photographs of the Indians are sold in book and postcard form at the **Casa Na Bolom Centre** (open Tues–Sun 4–7pm) at the upper end of Calle Vicente Guerrero. They are taken by Gertrude Blom, a Swiss photographer-anthropologist-ecologist and widow of the Maya expert Frans Blom, who has made her house a base for scholars and archaeologists for many years. You may visit the library, collections and shop. Don't leave town before a climb up **Cerro de San Cristóbal** (St Christopher's Hill) to visit the church here and admire the fine view over the city.

The Indian Villages of Chiapas

The nearby Indian villages certainly merit a detour and can be reached either by cab or *colectivo*. The best way to see the nearby villages is to meet up with one of the three local tour guides who take small groups to the towns. (Mercedes Hernández leaves from the zócalo around 9am. Alex and Raul leave from here also, around 9.30am, and Pepe leaves from Casa Na-Bolom around 10am.) These people are well informed about the customs of the towns, where the law of Mexico matters less than the law of the communities. Be very careful about photographing; several tourists have been injured by local men when they pulled out their cameras to take pictures.

The village of **San Juan Chamula** and especially its church must be seen. Inside, hundreds of candles set on a floor carpeted with pine needles provide both light and heat. You may see men facing the altar with a bottle on the floor in front of them. From time to time they will take a swig from their bottle – it is hard liquor and the act is ritual drinking. This ceremony, rooted in the Maya past, is to 'bring back the spirit' to a person who has lost his appetite for food or for life. The outward signs here are Christian, but Maya traditions lie just beneath the surface. It is forbidden to photograph in the church or during the dancing at festivals. Outside, the men in capes carrying staffs are the elected guardians of the shrine. It is an honour to have this responsibility, or cargo, even though it is expensive – the cargo officers have to pay for the festivals during the year of their service. As a footnote to history, note that San Juan de Chamula and its environs were given to the chronicler of the conquest, Bernal Díaz del Castillo.

Zinacantán, 5km (3 miles) farther on, is a ceremonial centre, also guarded by cargo officers. These villages are packed with dancers on feast days. (Inquire at the Tourist Information Office in San Cristóbal de las Casas for dates and times.) Horse-rides from town can be arranged. It is pleasant to walk one way, past small farms and orchards, by streams where women are doing the washing and through stretches of woodland, and then take the *colectivo* back.

The closest airport to San Cristóbal de las Casas is in the Chiapas capital, Tuxtla Gutiérrez. The 90-minute trip passes through mountainous terrain where coffee and flowers are grown. Off go the sweaters as you drop down to 530m (1,738ft). Short side trips off this road worth considering are

Worship in San Juan Chamula is a mix of Christian and Mayan tradition

to **Chiapa de Corzo**, 16km (10 miles) outside Tuxtla Gutiérrez. This very old village is famous for its lacquered masks and gourds, which are sold around the zócalo and in the shop of the small Museo de la Laca. The dammed Río Grijalva backs up into a lake and the spectacular narrow **Cañón del Sumidero**, with walls more than 1,000m (3,000ft) high. You can go by boat down the gorge and back from Chiapa de Corzo in a couple of hours, or view the fjord-like scenery from El Sumidero lookout on a road from Tuxtla Gutiérrez. (There are in fact two airports in Tuxtla Gutiérrez, one 25 minutes out of town and the other closer in. Which one is operating depends on the time of year. Be sure to find out which one your plane is leaving from.)

THE GULF COAST

Veracruz

Veracruz isn't on most tourist itineraries. Its residents tend to be unaffected, easy-going and very sure of themselves. They have a good time and will make room for visitors to share the fun, but don't make a big business of it. Veracruz has the best Carnival and maybe the worst handicraft market. It is steeped in history, but has few monuments. It was here that Cortés landed and burned his boats, here that Spanish dominion in Mexico ended three centuries later. The gold and silver galleons sailed for Spain from Veracruz, so it was a prime target for pirates. American marines and French *zouaves* invaded too. Today, as Mexico's principal seaport, the harbour is always filled with ships and tooting tugboats.

This is the background to keep in mind in Veracruz, but once you're here, the atmosphere will take over: just *being* here becomes more important than *doing* anything. A lot of time can be passed happily just sitting in a café, listening to the special beat of local music and imagining Humphrey

Colourful exuberance at Veracruz's famous Carnival

Bogart, unshaven and in a stained white linen suit, doing a deal with a shifty-eyed Peter Lorre at the next table. It's the archetypal tropical port you've seen in a hundred movies.

A look at the city could begin with a walk along the harbourside promenade, the Malecón, which is called 'El Boulevard' after it turns away from the harbour and runs south along the coast. Next to the Malecón is a plaza with a Stalinesque statue of President Venustiano Carranza, who briefly made Veracruz the capital of Mexico in 1914. Across the plaza stands a former lighthouse of the Carranza period. On the Malecón's broad esplanade tickets are sold for the boat trip out around the harbour and around the **Isla de Sacrificios**, the lighthouse island where some remains of sacrifices have been found. The short trip gives a breezy view of the city from the sea.

The **Mercado de Curiosidades** is at the very beginning of the Malecón. It is rightfully called the market of curios,

The state of Veracruz is home to the Totonac Indians

for the crafts tend to be tacky knick-knacks made of seashells, cheap scarves and plastic ship models. Across the street, on the Insurgentes section of the Malecón, ceiling fans stir the air in a block-long café as big as a bus station. This is **Café de la Parroquia**, an institution in this city, packed to overflowing at meal-times. Breakfast is especially nice to have here. Order a *café lechero* (coffee with milk) and you'll be served a glass with a couple of measures of strong black coffee at the bottom. Tap it with your spoon to get the attention of the waiters who circulate with kettles of hot foaming milk, which they pour with a great flourish.

Castello San Juan de Ulúa, the most interesting historical monument in Veracruz, lies across the harbour. You can go across by boat from the Malecón, or take a bus from a stop just north of the Palacio Municipal to this fort, now surrounded by the cranes and tracks of a container-ship dock and rail terminal. Built in the mid-18th century on the site of 16th-century fortifications, the bastion was the last

Under the dictatorship of Porfirio Díaz, San Juan de Ulúa was a high-security prison exclusively for political prisoners. Their living conditions were pitiful; at high tide, sea water rose waist-high in some cells.

Spanish foothold in Mexico. The Spanish fleet bombarded independence forces in Veracruz in 1822, when royalist refugees filled the fortress. It finally surrendered to a young Mexican officer named Antonio López de Santa Anna making his first mark on history.

The castle-fortress and its predecessors seem to have done little to protect Veracruz. The English privateers Francis Drake and John Hawkins took and retook the city in the late 1500s, and Dutch buccaneer Laurent de Graff, feared around the Gulf as 'Lorencillo', sacked and burned it for three days in 1683. The French bombarded the city twice, and the US three times, in 1847, 1914 and 1917. Small wonder that few monuments are left. In the 19th century San Juan de Ulúa was a notoriously horrible prison, with walls 2½m (8ft) thick and the sea for a moat. Carranza turned the prison headquarters into a presidential residence, but was assassinated before he could occupy it.

A local bus trundles along the Malecón in Veracruz

The **Museo Regional** (open Tues–Sun 10am–8pm), at 397 Calle Zaragoza, is worth visiting to sort out the turbulent history of the town. This is the only museum that documents the role of African slaves in Mexico. Cortés imported the first from Cape Verde to work his sugar plantations and in 1641 records showed 35,089 Africans in New Spain. Communities founded by escaped slaves near Acapulco still have a strong African strain and the Cuban-African influence in music and race is marked around Veracruz. A pronouncement abolishing slavery was one of the first acts of Father Hidalgo during the uprising of 1810, but slaves were not actually freed until the constitution of 1857.

The museum also has a small section about the pirates' attacks against the city and another on the epidemics that savaged Veracruz for much of its history, such as yellow fever and malaria. Another museum close by is installed in the **Baluarte de Santiago** (open Tues–Sun 10am–4.30pm), a remnant of the once formidable but ineffectual city battlements. Another is the **Museo de Historia Naval** (open Tues–Sun 9am–5pm), housed in the former naval academy, where you can get free guided tours that explain a lot of the

The Baluarte de Santiago, city fortifications built in 1526

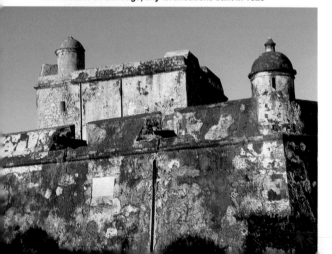

town's history as a port. The **Acuario** (aquarium) is one of the city's major attractions (open Mon–Thur 10am–7pm, Fri–Sun 10am–7.30pm).

The heart of Veracruz is the **Plaza de Armas**, perhaps the ◀ most lively square in the country. It is at its liveliest at night when the air is cool and families come out to stroll around. In front of the brightly lit Moorish-style city hall, the city's *danzonera* band starts playing at 8pm on Tuesdays, Thursdays and Saturdays. Couples dance the *danzón* on the elevated platform that many years ago held a bandstand similar to other plazas. Soon after the *danzón* different styles of music break out as itinerant musicians strike up their tunes – *mariachi* and *ranchero*, which now might be considered Mexico's national music; or *jarocha*, from the region just south of the port, from which originated *La Bamba*; or *marimba*, which probably came from Chiapas via Tabasco and is now much-loved here. Veracruzanos actually like any music that is cheerful and rhythmic, such as salsa. The activity in the plaza can last until 3am.

> The *danzón* was brought to Veracruz from Cuba in the 19th century, and Veracruzanos have made it their own. In it, couples alternate between a rumba-like dance and short promenades, during which the women wave beautiful hand-held fans.

Take a table at one of the cafés under the arches, order the food and beverage of your choice and sit back and watch the goings-on. Without moving from your table you have the opportunity to buy locally made or Cuban cigars, lottery tickets, seafood, articles of clothing, sunglasses and the ubiquitous chiclets. Most of the people at the surrounding tables will be locals and you can see how well they enjoy themselves. With all the hoopla, it's as if Carnival had never stopped.

A striking Olmec mask, in the Xalapa anthropology museum

Carnival, of course, is the main event of the year for the city. Hotel reservations have to be made well in advance. It is particularly popular with people from other parts of Mexico who view Veracruz society as being much less rigid and inhibited than society in the rest of the country. Carnival in Veracruz is for them an opportunity to go a little crazy. It begins on Shrove Tuesday in the zócalo with the burning of the effigy of *Mal Humor* (bad humour) and ends with the symbolic burial of 'Juan Carnival', accompanied by a morality play on the evils of drink and infidelity. Clubs work all year long on their costumes, bands and floats for parades.

Into the Mountains

The coastal hinterland between Veracruz and Villahermosa is the cradle of Mexican civilisation, the home of the Olmecs from 1200 to around 400BC. Little has survived of the cities they built of wood and mud brick in swampy, almost inaccessible areas. But the Olmecs left amazing works of art and influenced the cultures that followed.

To see a superb collection of these treasures, it is worth making the 96km (60-mile) trip to the state capital, **Xalapa** (*ha-LA-pa*, often spelled Jalapa). The road, which eventually reaches Puebla, winds up into cool highlands where you'll get a good view of the perpetual snows and perfect cone of the **Pico de Orizaba**, at 5,700m (18,551ft) the highest mountain in Mexico. Azaleas and camellias bloom in January in this cool mountain city of attractive, lush gardens. The light drizzle of the *chipi-chipi* rains keeps it refreshingly green.

The beautiful modern **Museo de Antropología** (Anthropology Museum, open daily 9am–5pm), a work of art in itself, is one of the most important in Mexico. In addition to the Olmec collection, it has a vast collection of the Totonac and Huastec cultures. The pieces that get the most attention, however, are six of the huge Olmec basalt 'helmeted' heads. They seem to have been transported to the Olmec cities at San Lorenzo, Tres Zapotes and La Venta, probably by raft, as far as 128km (80 miles) from the nearest quarry. Just as remarkable, the finely chiselled portraits were cut in the hard stone without metal tools. Yet after such effort, the heads were deliberately disfigured by the Olmecs and buried in the pits.

Indians working the fields, with the ruins of El Tajín beyond

The Olmecs worshipped a Jaguar God. Many figures in the museum are of a fanged half-human, half-animal 'were-jaguar'. A particularly moving sculpture is of a priest holding in his lap the limp body of a sacrificed child. Other sculptures show a realism that represents a departure from the Olmec stylisation. Also exhibited are the four-wheeled animal toys in clay; figures with the artificially deformed heads copied by the Maya; superb portraits in terracotta, some painted and with holes in the head for inserting hair or feathers; and a model of a ball game that shows that this ritual, too, originated with the Olmecs. There are also many of the curious laughing boys with flat triangular faces that belong to the Totonac culture. Surely this is one of the greatest museums of its kind.

The Xalapa museum contains a number of works from the Totonac city **El Tajín** in the northern part of the state. The remarkable feature of this important ruin is the **Templo de los Nichos**, a six-layered pyramid, pierced by closely set window-like niches. The architecture of all the buildings at this large site is unlike anything else in Mexico. Some of the Totonac pottery has scroll designs and tripod feet that are very much like Chinese vessels. The site is open daily 9am–5pm.

El Tajín is a few miles from **Papantla**, the vanilla-growing home town of the *voladores*, the men who go spinning around at the end of long ropes hanging from a tall pole. Since they perform all over the country, you need not make the day-long round trip from Veracruz to see them on their native ground. But it is too bad that El Tajín is so far off the beaten track, for it is well worth a visit. North of this region is the oil-producing and shipping area around Tampico and Poza Rica, and then the long road to the Texas border at Matamoros-Brownsville.

The Coast

Gulf Coast beaches aren't all that fantastic. The best at Veracruz is **Mocambo**, a resort with hotel gardens, pools and restaurants on a very broad, flat beach. The water is shallow a long way out. Farther on are **Boca del Río** and **Mandinga**, villages abounding in seafood restaurants and bars where *La Bamba* and similar *jarocha* songs are accompanied by the Veracruz 'harp' and guitars. 'Authentic' and

The flying men of Papantla: the *voladores* perform regularly at El Tajín

'seedy' are adjectives equally appropriate to these popular weekend retreats.

The spot where Cortés landed on 22 April 1519 is unmarked but presumed to be facing the little island of San Juan de Ulúa. The day was Good Friday; he later optimistically named his base **La Villa Rica de la Vera Cruz**, the 'Rich Town of the True Cross'. That base was moved several times, finally to the present city limits. The first town, just to the north, is now a village of cobbled streets, **La Antigua**, where the only monument is a bust of the national hero, Benito Juárez. About 40km (25 miles) north, off Route 180, are the ruins of **Zemopoala**, the **Totonac** city where Cortés recruited allies that were to be crucial to his battles with the Aztecs. There are five partly reconstructed pyramid-temples and bits and pieces of Totonac buildings throughout the modern town. At weekends you are likely to find the famous *voladores* who come here from Papantla.

WHAT TO DO

Whether you are a sportsman or a spectator, a golfer or a surfer, a lover of local arts and crafts or a devotee of *fiesta*, Mexico is a natural playground for the actively inclined. The range of diversions on offer in this country is as varied as its landscapes.

OUTDOOR ACTIVITIES

Watersports

Scuba diving and **snorkelling** on the Caribbean reefs are world-class, with Cozumel, Isla Mujeres and Cancún the most popular spots for year-round underwater activities.

Cozumel is one of the top 10 diving destinations in the world. The mainland side of the island offers the best diving, both in the national park at Palancar and in other diving sites such as Columbia, Paraíso and the spectacular wall diving at Santa Rosa. For more experienced divers, Maracaibo and Barracuda offer incredible sights and spectacular coral formations. Several of the sites for shallow dives, especially Palancar, Paraíso and Columbia, are also ideal for snorkelling. One of Cozumel's longest-standing dive shops offering tours and instruction is Aquaworld; tel: (987) 872-1210.

Isla Mujeres has good sites. Manchones reef, the closest at 1km (½ mile) out, is also ideal for snorkelling because of its shallow waters and great visibility. Another excellent snorkelling site is the Lighthouse Reef off the northwestern tip of the island, and if you want to snorkel from the shore there is the El Garrafón/Punta Sur national park at the southern tip. The most extraordinary diving experience from Isla Mujeres is the cave

Xcaret ecopark, south of Cancún

of the sleeping sharks where, between January and March, you can see nurse sharks floating and very still inside a sea cave. The dive shop with the longest-standing reputation on Isla Mujeres is Buzos de México, tel: (998) 877-0500; Sea Friends, on Playa Norte, is another good option, tel: (998) 842-5348.

Cancún is perfect for beginner divers and snorkellers, with numerous shallow diving sites. Punta Nizuc, the best site for diving, is also the northern tip of the Gran Arrecife Maya, the largest reef in the western hemisphere. The largest operator in Cancún is Aquaworld, tel: (998) 885-2288. Experienced divers can enjoy the unique experience of *cenote* diving in freshwater springs with cave formations; the largest cavern system, with access to snorkellers as well, is just north of Tulum; contact Hidden Worlds on tel: (984) 877-8535.

The Pacific coast offers its own treasures, with extraordinary diving sites off the shores of Los Cabos and Cabo Pulmo. Here

Diving in the flooded caverns north of Tulum

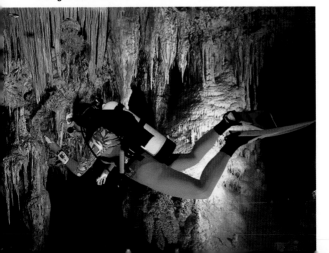

divers can enter an amazing submarine world with spectacular sand falls and encounter sealions, dolphins and even whale sharks. Most hotels and resorts offer reputable dive shops with certified divers and instructors.

Puerto Escondido has one of the world's best **surfing** beaches, and there's good surfing at San Blas as well. The best waves along the Mexican coast are caught during the autumn. Surfers seem to have their own network for

Kayaking off the Yucatán

information about the best beaches and hang-outs, so word-of-mouth is the best way to learn all the secrets. Another option is to contact Tropical Surf in Cruz de Juanacaxtle, tel: (329) 295-5087. It is easy to find operators offering **waterskiing**, **windsurfing**, **parasailing** and noisy little waverunners on the beaches of most hotels.

Sea-kayaking along the coastal inlets and islands of the Sea of Cortez is increasingly popular. The best areas are concentrated near La Paz and Loreto. In La Paz, contact Las Parras Tours, tel: (613) 135-1010; or Fenton's Sea Kayaking, tel: 1/135-3407. Both offer kayak lessons and tours that range in length from half a day to overnight. Loreto offers island exploration tours for beginner, intermediate and advanced kayakers. The tour can be customised to fit your needs and expectations, including camping by moonlight on deserted islands. Las Parras also offers the widest variety of sea-kayaking tours in Loreto, plus excellent advice regarding other outdoor activities in the area.

Deep-sea Fishing

Mazatlán, on the Pacific coast, has a reputation as one the best spots for marlin, tuna and yellowtail. Several fleets offer their services to fishermen from all over the world. The best season is October–January; rates go from around 1,600 pesos for a small outboard boat called a *panga* to close to 3,000 pesos for a private fishing charter on a 12½m (38ft) cruiser. It is best to contact an established fleet recommended by the tourism office in Mazatlán, tel: (669) 916-5160.

Adventure Tourism

Mexico's rugged terrain and varied landscape provides the perfect backdrop for vigorous exploration. The Mexican Association of Adventure Travel and Ecotourism (AMTAVE) offers the most complete information about ecotourism and adventure tours, with around 40 travel providers, website: <www.amtave.com>.

Hiking and backpacking in the Copper Canyon area take you into real wilderness; the best way to enjoy these wonderful and physically demanding trails is to hire an experienced guide or contact an organiser to arrange transport, lodging and hiking. Two companies with excellent options for serious hikers and backpackers are Naturequest <www.naturequesttours.com> and Wildland Adventures <www.wildland.com>.

The Sierra Madre Mountains near to Puerto Vallarta provide challenging and easily accessible **hiking** and **mountain biking** excursions. Bike-Mex offers expert guided tours into the mountains and other outlying areas, tel: (322) 223-1834. Take part in a thrilling rafting excursion or kayak down the gorge of the Usumacinta River, or the numerous rivers in the state of Veracruz. In Xalapa, Veraventuras offers the most options for rafting along the different rivers in the state, with tours for all levels of expertise, tel: (228) 818-9779; website: <www.veraventuras.com.mx>. For information about trips to the Usumacinta river, check the Chiapas tourism office website: <www.turis-mochiapas. gob.mx>.

Golf

Golfers will find courses in good to excellent condition in almost every resort and all major cities in Mexico. Most courses have carts and clubs for hire. Los Cabos has become the country's golf Mecca, with world-class courses that are equal or superior to those found in

Pok Ta Pok golf course in Cancún

other countries, not least for the scenery they offer. Green fees range between 300 and 2,500 pesos.

The northern Pacific coast has several championship courses between Puerto Vallarta and Manzanillo, all with exceptional coastal views and uncrowded fairways. A Jack Nicklaus course, just north of Puerto Vallarta at the Four Seasons Punta Mita, has a spectacular hole that drives to a natural island 160m (175yds) offshore. The region around Puerto Vallarta has a total of six courses, including one public course.

South along the coast known as the Costa Alegre, spectacular courses offer exclusive play and oceanside vistas at Isla Navidad, one of Mexico's top-rated resort courses, and El Tamarindo. Green fees at these regional golf courses range between 400 and 1,600 pesos for 18 holes. In Manzanillo, La Mantarray golf course at the Las Hadas resort is considered among the most scenic in the world, with its million-dollar island green on the 18th hole. Green fees on these courses range between 750 and 1,200 pesos.

Tennis

All resorts have good tennis courts, with a variety of surfaces that include clay and grass. Two of the best resorts for tennis facilities are Puerto Vallarta and Loreto. Puerto Vallarta has two top-class tennis centres: the Canto del Sol Plaza, located in the Hotel Continental Plaza, offers eight courts, four covered and four clay; and the Iguana Tennis Center, just off the highway before the entrance to Marina Vallarta, has three courts, one outdoor and two covered with Astroturf surfaces. In Loreto, you can play tennis at the Centro Tenístico Loreto – also known as the John McEnroe Tennis Center – adjacent to the Eden Resort, with nine lighted asphalt courts. Court fees across Mexico range between 75 and 180 pesos per hour. Most tennis courts offer racket hire at between 25 and 50 pesos.

Spectator Sports

There's **greyhound racing** every day at Agua Caliente in Tijuana and **horse racing** Friday, Saturday and Sunday in Mexico City. Betting is also part of the excitement in Acapulco, at the courts called *frontones*, where jai-alai is played. In this lightning-fast Basque version of handball, players whip the ball with wicker scoops strapped to their hands.

Charreadas, a Mexican kind of **rodeo** organised by horsemen's clubs, are held almost every Sunday noon at several rings in Mexico City, in Guadalajara and on occasion in other cities of the north.

The art of **bullfighting** inspires extremes: some see it as unacceptably cruel animal torture, while others esteem it as a richly symbolic drama involving grace and courage. Whatever your opinion, the *corridas de toros* are an important, even essential, part of Mexico's culture. There are 225 permanent bullrings in the country, and around 500 improvised arenas. In Mexico City, the 50,000-seat Plaza Mexico, off Insurgentes Sur, is the world's largest bullring. The programme starts punctually at 4pm every Sunday from October to March. For ticket information, go to the Plaza on Saturday morning, or call, tel: (55) 5563-3961.

The livelier crowd sits in the sunny section *sección de sol*, though the seats in the covered section are cooler in the afternoon sun. If you really want to feel the thrill of the corrida, splurge and get *barrera* tickets – these are the closest to the ring, but note that they are not for those who have mixed feelings about the *Fiesta Brava*. In *barreras* you hear the bull, you smell the blood and you taste the dust as the bull charges.

Young rodeo riders

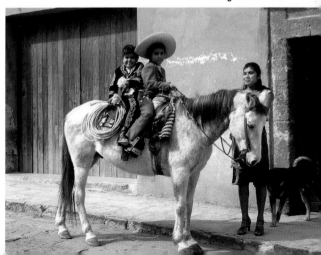

SHOPPING

The best shopping in Mexico is for handcrafted *artesanía*, decorative objects and, thanks to the rich mineral mines of Mexico's mountains, silver jewellery. Each region in Mexico has its own specialities; in each, artisan traditions are handed down from generation to generation and blend the area's unique mix of indigenous and Spanish roots.

Handicrafts

Regional crafts include pottery of all kinds, glazed and often painted in designs unique to each locale; hand-blown

Pottery from Dolores Hidalgo

glassware from Jalisco state; naïve paintings on bark or stitched in yarn from Morelos and Nayarit; wildly exuberant Adam and Eve 'Tree of Life' candelabra from the states of Mexico and Puebla; grotesque masks used in traditional indigenous ceremonies; whimsical, colourful animals made of carved wood and papier mâché, called *alebrijes*, from Oaxaca; exquisite lacquerware from Olinala, in Guerrero and Michoacán; and straw products, from baskets to Panama-style hats, found in coastal regions. Basketry is also a speciality in the Copper Canyon area.

Found across the country are wood-carved boxes; toys and Christmas tree ornaments in painted tin; nutshells housing tiny figures and miniature doll furniture; *maracas* made from gourds that are carved, painted and lacquered; and *piñatas*, the candy-filled papier-mâché balloons in fanciful shapes.

> As you shop, be aware that certain items are made from protected species. It is illegal to sell tortoiseshell and black coral products – both of which are also illegal to import into the EU, the US and Australia.

For the collector, genuine colonial antiques can be found, as well as excellent copies. Mexico City's Bazaar Sábado is an excellent place to search.

Silver and Jewellery

Silver jewellery, picture frames and ornaments can be a bargain (but buy only those with the '925' stamp, denoting true silver). There are beautifully crafted vessels of copper, plus mirrors, lanterns and chandeliers of ornamental tin.

Mexican opals, turquoise, lapis lazuli, onyx and other semi-precious stones and minerals are widely available and downright cheap. The silver capital is Taxco, but shops throughout the country feature fine Mexican silver.

Clothing

Look out for fine, hand-woven woollen *sarapes* (a kind of poncho), from Saltillo and Oaxaca; cotton, wool or silk shawls of many colours, called *rebozos*, from San Luis Potosí; rugs in Indian designs; *huipiles*, the square-cut embroidered blouses worn by indigenous women throughout Mexico; and *guayaberas*, box-cut men's shirts, with pleats and some embroidery, made popular in the Yucatán, Campeche, Tabasco and Veracruz.

Leather goods such as *huarache* sandals, belts, jackets, wallets, handbags and hats are especially popular in León and Guadalajara. The tooled-leather saddles and boots are Mexican works of art, known as *Piteado*, and created in Jalisco.

Where to Shop

Wherever you go in Mexico there will be a market, and in every market you will find local handicrafts. The government's handicrafts foundation (FONART) has shops at several places in Mexico City and in major tourist centres. Officials from FONART scour the countryside and buy direct from artisans in order to offer the highest quality at the fairest price. In Mexico City, the main location is on Patriotismo 691, open daily 9am–8pm, and a branch at Avenida Juarez 89, near the Alameda, open Mon–Sat 10am–7pm. There are also FONART stores in Morelia, San Luis Potosí, Oaxaca and Tlaquepaque. For details, go to <www.fonart. gob.mx> and click on *Directorio de centros de acopio*.

The municipal and state governments also operate Mercados, Centros de Artesanías and the fixed-price shops found in many museums around the country. If you want to take your shopping seriously, it's useful to check the prices, quality and variety of goods in these places to compare for bargaining in the public markets and craft shops.

In the capital and major resorts, crafts from every part of the country are sold in markets. This is good to know when you're grinding your teeth over a missed opportunity in Pátzcuaro or Oaxaca. But it's more fun to buy your finds from the source, all the more so to see them being made by weavers and potters. You'll find more variety at the source, too, though prices won't be much lower. Increased demand due to mass tourism has definitely lowered standards. Shop around and don't hesitate to point out what competing shops and stalls are offering. You may find, too, that established handicraft shops, while costing more, offer better quality than the big *artesanía* markets.

ENTERTAINMENT

The most dynamic entertainment is found in Mexico City and in the resort areas. The big city nightlife mirrors that of Spain, with clubs of live music and dancing staying open very late and night-owl cafés. In Cancún, the clubs are primarily predictable, world-renowned chains, located in grand entertainment and shopping centres. Cabo San Lucas, despite its recent gentrification, still maintains an outlaw-style nightlife, with a row of rowdy bars open until it's time to head out fishing again.

In Puerto Vallarta, a respectable live music scene has emerged, with a collection of clubs within walking distance of one another that play everything from the blues to mariachi. No resort is better known for sizzling nightlife than Acapulco, with its dazzling cliffside discos and more casual but dynamic bars that line the waterfront along the main drag; you'll also

Mariachi musician

For tickets for the Ballet Folklórico and information (in Spanish) call the Palacio de Bellas Artes on (55) 5512-2593. For advance purchase, call Ticketmaster, an electronic ticketing service, tel: (55) 5325-9000. Another way to arrange tickets is through your hotel's travel agency – they will probably provide good seats and pick you up at your hotel.

find a healthy selection of Cuban salsa clubs, chorus lines of female impersonators, an active red-light district – it's all here.

Mexico City's Ballet Folklórico de México puts on a show that everyone wants to see at least once. The chance to see its home near the Alameda, the Palacio de Bellas Artes, is alone worth the price of admission. The programme recreates pre-Hispanic dances as well as Mexico's wonderfully varied regional music and fiestas, with gorgeous costumes. The ballet performs year-round on Wednesdays at 8.30pm and Sundays at 9.30am and 8.30pm – although the Sunday evening performance is frequently cancelled to accommodate other events. Touring companies of the ballet also often perform in Acapulco, Cancún and other cities.

The provinces have quite good ballets of their own, too – Mérida's is one of the best. If you're in Oaxaca the last two Mondays in July, get tickets to the Guelaguetza, held in the amphitheatre on the Cerro del Fortín overlooking the city, in which dances of the state's seven regions are performed in native costumes, including the huge feather headdress of the Danza de las Plumas. Tickets are available through the state tourism office, tel: (951) 516-0994 or (951) 514-2155. You should buy your tickets well in advance in order to guarantee a space. Throughout Mexico, traditional entertainment accompanies all major holidays and the innumerable local fiestas. And every resort hotel worth the salt on its margarita glasses has a 'Fiesta Mexicana' night at least once a week.

Beautiful 100-year-old theatres have been restored in the Silver Cities and Oaxaca. Concerts, opera, musicals and stage plays are performed regularly in these gilt-and-velvet halls. Important cultural festivals, such as the October Cervantes Festival in Guanajuato, attract artists from around the world. This festival brings together performances of theatre; classical, modern and folkloric dance; and classical, folkloric, jazz and rock concerts, featuring an international roster of talent. The city itself becomes the stage, with venues in all the plazas, theatres and streets. The cultural institutions of San Miguel de Allende, Guadalajara, Cuernavaca, Puebla and Morelia frequently schedule concerts and other performances that you may enjoy even if you don't speak Spanish. Check the listings magazine *Tiempo Libre* and local tourist information offices for details.

Dancing at the weekly *Mérida en Domingo* fiesta

For informal entertainment, go to the *zócalo* in any city or town any evening around 8pm – especially on Sundays – and you'll probably find a band or a marimba orchestra on the bandstand going all-out for an appreciative crowd. Often there will be dancing. In Mérida a regular schedule of varied musical performances takes place in a different plaza every night. In Veracruz, the music goes on from mid-morning until late at night, with couples frequently dancing the sultry *danzón* in the Plaza de Armas and the Parque Zamora.

The Plaza Garibaldi in Mexico City and Plaza de los Mariachis in Guadalajara seem never to sleep, with mariachi music playing non-stop. The mariachis congregate here and play, in an attempt to be hired out for a party. The atmosphere is festive and it's a great way to hear a makeshift concert of this traditional music.

Traditional dress for the Festival of the Virgin of Guadalupe

Fiestas

Somewhere in Mexico, you can be sure that a fiesta is under way right now. This has to be true, because every occupation and day of the year has a patron saint, because everybody has a birthday to share with neighbours and friends, because the seasons and the stars have always demanded recognition of their changes. Oaxaca even has a 'Night of the

Radishes', on 23 December, when the zócalo is surrounded by stalls of long red radishes carved into figures.

Where but in Mexico do families stage an all-night vigil by the grave of a departed loved one while picnicking and eating skull-shaped candies? The famed Day of the Dead festivities (Día de los Muertos – *see page 103*) take place throughout the country on 1–2 November

**Papier-mâché skeletons
celebrate the Day of the Dead**

every year, but nowhere are they more visually moving than in Janitzio and the villages surrounding Pátzcuaro in Michoacán.

Mexico celebrates, with varying degrees of intensity, 13 official national holidays and 352 unofficial ones. Add one more for Leap Year and don't count on the unofficial ones being celebrated on the same day each year – if a fiesta falls in midweek, some towns might decide to stretch the holiday to three or four days to include the nearest weekend.

None of the national holidays has religious significance, with the exception of Christmas and Easter. Yet all the most important fiestas follow the Roman Catholic calendar. A celebration that begins with Mass at the church may move into the plaza afterwards as masked dancers carry on ancient Indian rites. Only anthropologists really care about such matters – for participants a fiesta is a fiesta: a time for dressing up, marching in parades, decorating the zócalo with strings of lights or garlands of paper, setting off fireworks, eating, drinking, dancing and being together with the whole family. In most cases, visitors can join in, but in some Indian villages, photography of rites is not allowed and onlookers should watch discreetly.

Calendar of Events

New Year's Day National holiday with parades, parties and fireworks everywhere.

6 January Epiphany: the day when children receive Christmas presents.

2 February Candlemas: music, dances, processions, food and other festivities lead up to a blessing of seed and candles in a tradition that mixes pre-Hispanic and European traditions marking the end of winter.

February/March Carnaval: revelry for the three days preceding Ash Wednesday and the beginning of Lent. Celebrated with special gusto in Tepoztlán, Huejotzingo, Chamula, Veracruz, Cozumel and Mazatlán.

19 March, San José del Cabo Feast of San José, the town's patron saint: street parties, dancing, horse races and food stalls.

21 March Benito Juárez's birthday: small home-town celebrations countrywide, especially in Juárez's birthplace – Guelatao, in Oaxaca state.

21 March, Chichén Itzá On the spring equinox, the shadow of the plumed serpent moves slowly down from the top of the Temple of Kukulcán; visitors from afar come to marvel at this sight.

Holy Week All of Mexico celebrates from Palm Sunday to Easter Sunday. Businesses close during this week of national holiday.

April, Mexico City Festival del Centro Histórico: three-week cultural extravaganza in the Old Town.

April–May, Aguascalientes San Marcos national fair, Mexico's largest, begins the third week in April and lasts 22 days.

April/May, Cuernavaca Flower festival

1 May Labour Day: workers parade countrywide and everything closes.

5 May Cinco de Mayo: national holiday that celebrates the defeat of the French at the Battle of Puebla in 1862.

1 June Día de la Marina (Navy Day): national holiday.

June, Tlaquepaque National Ceramics Fair and Fiesta on the outskirts of Guadalajara offers craft demonstrations, competitions and more.

14 June Our Lady of Carmen: fiestas in Catemaco and Ciudad del Carmen.

July (last two Mondays), Oaxaca Guelaguetza Dance Festival: one of Mexico's most popular events.

August, Puerto Escondido International surfing competition.

1–15 August, San Miguel de Allende The International Chamber Music Festival features international classical music ensembles.

13 August, Mexico City Wreath-laying ceremonies in the Plaza de las Tres Culturas commemorate the Fall of Tenochtitlán to Cortés.

15 August Assumption of the Virgin Mary: many towns have festivals, notably Huamantla, Tlaxcala.

1–15 September, Guadalajara Public concerts of mariachi music performed by groups from around the world, plus workshops and lectures on the history, culture and music of the mariachi in Mexico.

15–16 September Independence Day: celebrates Mexico's independence from Spain with parades, picnics and fiestas throughout the country. At 11pm on 15 September, the president of Mexico gives the famous independence *grito* (shout) from the national palace in Mexico City.

21 September, Chichén Itzá The same shadow play that occurs during the spring equinox repeats itself for the autumn equinox.

October–November, Guanajuato The Cervantes Festival attracts performing artists from all over the world.

October, Guadalajara Fiestas de Octubre: a month of popular culture, fine arts and mariachi music.

Days of the Dead All Saints' Day, 1 November, honours saints and deceased children; All Souls' Day, 2 November, honours deceased adults. Relatives gather at cemeteries with candles and food, often spending the night beside graves of loved ones.

November, Puerto Vallarta Fiesta del Mar: a month of activities including art, sports, the Mexico boat show and a gourmet dining festival.

November–December, Taxco National Silver Fair: exhibits, concerts and fireworks celebrate Mexico's best silversmiths.

12 December The Virgin of Guadalupe, the patron saint of Mexico, is honoured with processions, Masses, street fairs, dancing and fireworks.

Christmas Mexicans extend this celebration and leave their jobs, often beginning two weeks before Christmas all the way through to New Year. Querétaro has a huge parade, Oaxaca has its 'Night of the Radishes'.

New Year's Eve Nationwide parties, fireworks and festivities.

EATING OUT

Mexican cuisine rates as one of the world's most varied and unusual. It is a cuisine with many regional variations, but a number of generalities can be made about it. The first thing to note is that Mexican food relies on the same basic ingredients used in pre-Columbian times: corn, beans, a wide variety of peppers (called chiles), tomatoes, squash and avocado.

The corn is boiled with lime, allowed to sit, then drained, rinsed and ground into a dough (*masa*). This is made into *tortillas* by pressing it into very thin circles and cooking it on a hot, seasoned griddle – usually a large, concave pan called a *comal*. The *masa* can also be formed into thicker cakes and cooked on the griddle, then opened and stuffed. Or it can be combined with other ingredients and wrapped and steamed to make *tamales*.

Tamales are an excellent example of regional variation. In northern Mexico and Texas they are small, have a lot of meat in them and are wrapped in a corn husk. In central Mexico, they are larger and have a lot more *masa* that has been worked until it is very light. In the Huasteca region, *tamales* are so big that one can feed a family of eight. In Michoacán, they make a *tamale* that has no filling and is wrapped in a corn leaf and another that is made of fresh corn rather than dried corn. In southern Mexico, they are wrapped in banana leaves and spiced with herbs not used elsewhere.

Many elements of today's Mexican cuisine were unknown here before the arrival of the Spanish – typical Mediterrranean food-stuffs such as chicken, pork and beef, cheese, wheat, olive oil, wine, onion and garlic.

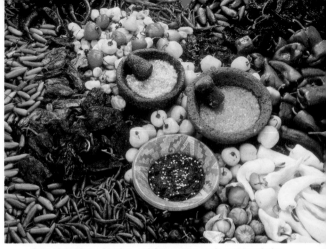
Colourful chiles – Mexican cuisine uses more than 100 varieties

To contrast with the spiciness of the other dishes, beans are cooked and served with the main course or afterwards. In Mexican households, once the pot of beans has been around for a couple of days, the beans are mashed and fried; these are called *frijoles refritos* (refried beans) and are usually served with breakfast or supper. Restaurants, however, now serve them at any meal.

Chiles – another distinguishing feature of Mexican cooking – are known by one name when they are fresh and another when dry. Drying can completely change the character of a chile: a fresh *chile poblano* has a mild, tangy flavour; when dry (*chile ancho*) it has a pungent, rich, earthy taste. Some chiles are very hot and with little flavour (*chile de árbol, chile pequín, chile habanero*), others are milder but have a strong flavour (*chile poblano, chile guajillo, chile cascabel*). One chile, the famous *jalapeño* (when smoked, it's called *chile chilpotle*), has a strong flavour and is very hot as well.

Meals

Breakfast (*el desayuno*) in Mexico can be either light or heavy. If eaten really early, it usually consists only of *café con leche* (coffee with milk) or hot chocolate and a piece of sweet bread. When eaten around 9 or 10 in the morning, it consists of a dish of eggs and tortillas cooked in a variety of ways, with fried beans, chile sauce, a plate of fruit and coffee and juice. Mexican egg dishes include *huevos rancheros* – eggs that are poached or fried and served on a tortilla in a smoothly blended, spicy, tomato-based sauce. *Huevos a la mexicana* are eggs scrambled with onion, tomato and hot *chiles serranos*. *Chilaquiles* are tortillas that are dried or toasted and cooked in a red or green sauce with chicken and onion, and usually come with a little crumbled cheese and cream on top.

The **main meal** of the day in Mexico (*la comida*) is taken between 2 and 4pm, though this is giving way in the big cities to lighter and faster meals for workers. (The afternoon siesta, which traditionally follows, has also been a casualty of the same forces.) The *comida* usually begins with an appetiser or salad, and then a soup or rice dish, known as *la sopa*. Mexicans make very good soups that rarely disappoint. Afterwards comes the main course, or *plato fuerte*, a meat or fish dish, and then dessert and coffee. The most common dessert is *flan*, which is an egg custard very similar to the French *crème caramel* only with more body, and is often flavoured with coconut or rum.

Grilled fish with salad

Supper (*la cena*) is taken around 8 o'clock or later. It is most often a small meal featuring some form of *antojitos*, which literally translated, means 'little cravings'. These dishes include *tacos*, simple *enchiladas*, *tortas*, *tostadas*, *chalupas*, *gorditas* and a variety of others depending on where you are in Mexico. *Antojitos* usually are a big hit with visitors to Mexico who often want something to eat that's faster than a full meal.

It is quite common for Mexicans to have **snacks** in the late morning or late afternoon. Common snack foods are some of the above-mentioned *antojitos*, espe-

A typical taco – meat, onion and coriander wrapped in a tortilla

cially *tacos*. A *taco* is anything wrapped in a tortilla. The tortilla is usually soft, but it can also be fried. Most tacos have some sort of meat in them and are topped with chopped onion and cilantro (fresh coriander leaves) with sauces on the side. Most commonly found is the *taco al pastor*, which is pork marinated in the intensely red sauce of ground *achiote* seed (annatto), sour orange and pineapple. Another great snack is the *licuado*, which is any fruit blended with ice and either water or milk. These are quite satisfying. Mexico is rich in a variety of tropical fruits, including mango, mamey, guayaba, zapote, papaya, chirimoya and guanábana, as well as the more familiar coconut, banana and orange.

Restaurants

Mexico has such a wonderful climate that it's no wonder that Mexicans enjoy eating outdoors. The many open-air restaurants in Mexico are often in the courtyards of colonial mansions or former convents, or under the stone archways that surround a plaza.

Whether indoors or outdoors, restaurants that cater for office workers and businesspeople tend to have, in addition to the regular menu items, a fixed-price, multi-course daily special for the large afternoon meal. This is called either a *comida corrida* or *menú del día*. It's your best bet for an inexpensive full meal.

Dishes that you might see on a restaurant menu include *mole*, of which there is a wide variety. The best known is

Maguey Spirits

Tequila is made by fermenting juice extracted from the heart of the blue *maguey*, an agave plant. A cluster of thick leaves a couple of metres tall rise from the ground around a spike that flowers at the top. In the centre of the flower, like the heart of an artichoke, is the pineapple-shaped core, the *piña*, which is cut out, roasted and squeezed to extract juice. When this is fermented and aged, it becomes tequila. True tequila is limited by government regulation to liquor produced in the provinces around Guadalajara.

Mezcal, a speciality of Oaxaca and certain regions of central Mexico, is made from the juice of other maguey plants but in much the same way. Mezcal has a stronger smell and taste. Both tequila and mezcal are around 76° proof. When aged, these liquors may be labelled *añejo* or *viejo*, and will have a golden colour.

Pulque is the traditional drink of the peasant in central Mexico. It is the fermented juice of a couple of species of agave, and is white, sweetish and slightly thick. It should be consumed as fresh as possible.

mole poblano, a dark brown, rich sauce made of ground chiles, toasted tortillas, bitter chocolate and several spices, served over chicken or turkey and sprinkled with sesame seeds. Also, there is *pipián verde*, a sauce made of ground pumpkin seeds among other ingredients; it is served on poultry as well. Another classic is *puerco en adobado*, in which pork is

Tequila, Mexico's national tipple

marinated in a rich sauce made with two to three varieties of dried *chiles* and then cooked slowly.

If you enjoy meat dishes that are slightly sweet, and you feel like splurging on calories, order a *chile en nogada* (providing it's in season). This is one of the most baroque of Mexican dishes – a *chile poblano* stuffed with a mixture of ground chicken, pork, raisins and almonds covered in a walnut cream sauce (in which the walnuts have had the thin brown skin removed so there is no bitterness) and sprinkled with pomegranate seeds.

Fish dishes in Mexico are outstanding, and include *huachinango a la veracruzana*, red snapper in tomato sauce with olives, capers and onions, *pescado al cilantro,* any fish in a tangy sauce of green tomatoes and coriander, or *al mojo de ajo,* fish sautéed with little pieces of garlic.

To accompany your meal, there is a wide variety of Mexican beers. Coffee is most often served American-style, but you can get it prepared in the traditional fashion of *café de olla* (cooked in an earthenware pot and spiced with cinnamon, cloves and raw brown sugar) or as espresso. Tequila, of course, is the national tipple. A final thing to know about dining out in Mexico is that waiters will not want to appear unwelcoming and so will not bring the bill until you've asked for it and even then will not bring it very quickly. If you're pressed for time, ask for your bill in advance. So enjoy yourself, and as Mexicans say when seeing others eat, '*¡Buen provecho!*' (may it do you good).

To Help You Order...

Here are a few terms that may enhance your dining experiences. Be bold and try to scrape by in Spanish – your efforts will be appreciated.

Do you have a table for one/ two/three/four people?	**¿Tiene una mesa para una/ dos/tres/cuatro persona/ personas?**
Do you have a menu?	**¿Tiene un menú?**
The bill, please	**La cuenta, por favor**

...and Read the Menu

aguacate avocado

ajo garlic

alcachofas artichokes

ate fruit paste usually made of guava or quince

atole sweet drink made with corn dough

bistek steak

café coffee

café con leche black coffee served with steamed milk

calamares squid

camarones shrimp

cebolla onion

cerdo/puerco pork

cerveza beer

chilaquiles corn tortillas cooked in a sauce of chiles

chorizo spicy pork sausage

consomé clear broth

enchiladas tortillas filled with chicken or cheese, with *mole*, tomato or green sauce

ensalada salad

flan sweet custard made with eggs, milk and vanilla

frijoles beans

horchata water flavoured with rice and almonds

huevos eggs

mariscos seafood

mejillones mussels

pan bread

papas potatoes

pescado fish

pollo chicken

pozole stew with maize and pork and/or chicken

quesadilla tortilla filled with cheese, other fillings

queso cheese

rajas poblano peppers with cream and cheese

res beef

salsa mexicana hot sauce made with tomatoes, green chiles, onions, coriander

salsa roja hot sauce made with red chiles and tomato

salsa verde sauce made with green peppers and green tomatoes

sopa soup

sopa de lima chicken broth flavoured with lime wedges, served with pieces of chicken

taco corn or flour tortilla stuffed with any number of fillings

tamal corn batter with sweet or savoury fillings, wrapped in corn husks and steamed

Sanborns restaurant in the Casa de los Azulejos, Mexico City

HANDY TRAVEL TIPS

An A–Z Summary of Practical Information

A

ACCOMMODATION (*Alojamiento*) (See also CAMPING, YOUTH HOSTELS)

Prices don't always tell the whole story of what to expect from a hotel in Mexico. A charming hotel in an old mansion may charge lower rates simply because it doesn't have TVs or a pool, while run-of-the-mill hostelries that feature such amenities may cost twice as much. Also, depending on the various package deals available and seasonal discounts, the same room may go for very different prices. As a rule, rates at the beaches and other resorts are higher from mid-December until Easter. In most cases you'll need to reserve in advance during this popular period. Any time of year, travellers arriving without reservations will find hotel information desks and phones in the major airports. The most economical accommodation can usually be found in small hotels near the central part of the city, or around the zócalo and in the older parts of a town. If you plan to spend a few weeks in Mexico at one place, you may want to rent an apartment; try looking in the local newspapers or call the local tourist information office, which can usually direct you to the most reliable places.

I'd like a single/double room with bath/shower.	**Quisiera una habitación sencilla/doble con baño/regadera.**
What's the rate per night?	**¿Cuál es la tarifa por noche?**
Where is there a cheap hotel?	**¿Dónde hay un hotel económico?**

AIRPORTS

Benito Juárez International Airport in Mexico City is actually inside the city limits. Seven national and 16 international airlines use the facilities, which may appear to be a great buzzing confusion at first, but are quite easy to navigate. Follow the signs to your luggage pickup point (*entrega de equipajes*), which will be area E for international flights and A for most national arrivals. When arriving on an international flight, you will clear immigration, which is on the same level as the arrival gates, and then go downstairs to claim your luggage. In the international arrival area, you may use one of the trolleys that are available at no charge in the baggage claim area to take your luggage to the customs clearance area, but not beyond; once you exit, porters will be waiting to help you to your taxi. Tip about 10 pesos per bag. Clearance through customs is fairly quick.

In the long hall outside the luggage areas, you will find banks and *casas de cambio* (private moneychangers, who give almost the same rate as a bank), where you can buy and sell your dollars and pesos. There are souvenir shops, bookstores and newsstands, places to eat and drink, hotel and travel information services, a post office (near Area A), one hotel inside the terminal and another linked to the terminal by a walkway, luggage lockers (*depósito de equipajes*) and many other useful services. If you need help, go to one of the information booths.

In more or less all cities of Mexico, yellow and white (mostly white) vehicles marked *transportación terrestre* are pre-paid inside the airport or just outside on the pavement. (These taxis are authorised and safe. Pay no attention to people calling 'Taxi!' or to anyone offering guide services.) When you get to the head of the line tell the dispatcher your destination, which he will relay to the cab driver. Give your pre-paid ticket to the driver, then sit back and relax.

There is a US$12 airport departure tax; most airlines include this tax in the price of your ticket, but double-check to make sure you are not caught by surprise at the airport when you leave.

Porter!	**¡Maletero!**
Where's the bus for…?	**¿Dónde se toma el camión para…?**

B

BARGAINING

Street and market vendors are prepared to bargain. As a rule of thumb, you should start by offering about 20 percent less than you are willing to pay. However you shouldn't enter into the haggling game unless you are really ready to buy, and never propose a price that is insultingly low. You can always break off a deadlock in a pleasant way, saying '*gracias*', and indicating that you want to look around. When you come back, you'll probably be able to knock at least 20 percent off the asking price without shedding blood.

How much is that?	**¿Cuánto es?**
Is there a discount?	**¿Me hace una rebaja?**

BUDGETING FOR YOUR TRIP

Value is the operative word when travelling to Mexico, and is among the country's principal appeals. You can find great bargains throughout the country, especially in colonial cities, coastal villages and smaller towns, but in Mexico City and well-developed resort areas as well. While you can encounter hotels that charge more than 1,500 pesos per night, budget-conscious travellers can find clean and comfortable accommodation ranging between 250 and 400 pesos per room per night. These rooms are usually for two persons and it is very common for children to be able to stay for free in their parents' room. Dining is excellent value when compared with most US or European destinations, with a *comida corrida* (a fixed-price lunch) costing between 25 and 35 pesos for a full meal with soup, rice or pasta, a main course, dessert, fruit-flavoured water, coffee and bread or tortillas. Breakfast and dinner can be just as inexpensive. Travel is also inexpensive, with bus journeys within a city rarely costing more than 5 pesos and a long, 1,200km (720-mile) trip costing around 700 pesos.

C

CAMPING

There are campsites throughout the country, including two in the vicinity of Mexico City itself. Most of the organised sites are found in the northern states and along the Pacific Coast, down to the state of Jalisco. Some hotels have places for camping as well. While it is usually safe to camp on most beaches, it is a good idea to take as many precautions as possible (ask locals about any regulations and safety). For information about camping in Mexico and a complete list of camping grounds and trailer parks in Mexico, contact INFOTUR: Presidente Mazaryk 172, Col. Polanco, México, DF, CP 11587, tel: 800-903-9200 or (55) 5250-0123.

May we camp here?	**¿Podemos acampar aquí?**
We have a tent/trailer	**Tenemos una tienda de campaña/un trailer**

CAR HIRE (*Arrendamiento de automóviles*) (See also DRIVING)

To hire a car the driver must be at least 21 years of age. All well-known international companies and many reliable national ones hire to adults with a valid driving licence and a credit card. Shop around for the best deal, but keep in mind that car hire is not a bargain in Mexico, because cars and their upkeep in general are more expensive here than they are elsewhere. Rates vary, but you can expect to pay between 350 and 750 pesos per day with unlimited mileage; it is advisable to take the insurance included option.

I'd like to hire a car	**Quisiera rentar un coche**
for today/tomorrow	**para hoy/mañana**
for one day/one week	**por un día/una semana**

CLIMATE

Mexico is a vast country with varied topography and a great variety of climates within its territory. Coastal regions enjoy summer-like, almost tropical weather practically year round, with temperatures ranging between 22° and 32°C (72° and 90°F), with rainy seasons usually running between June and November. Winter mornings and evenings can be cool, especially along the Baja coast and most northern beach destinations. Mexico City and other inland colonial cities are cool in the winter, with temperatures occasionally dropping below 10°C (50°F), and pleasantly warm during spring and summer, with temperatures reaching the mid 20s C (70s F); however, evenings and mornings are almost always cool.

CLOTHING

The lightest and most informal summer clothing is fine for all the beach resorts year-round, but you should bring a light sweater and windbreaker for the occasional cool mornings and evenings; also keep in mind that at high altitudes and in the desert, winter temperatures can dip quite low. A raincoat or umbrella will come in handy from May to October. Ties and jackets for men are virtually unknown at beach resorts but are commonly worn in the better restaurants of the big cities, particularly in the evening. Don't wear extra-short miniskirts or shorts (the latter goes for men as well) anywhere in Mexico apart from the big tourist resorts. As a general rule, in the more remote villages both men and women should take care to dress conservatively. A comfortable pair of walking shoes (for scrambling over ruins and pyramids) are a must.

COMPLAINTS (*Reclamación*)

If you have a complaint against a hotel, restaurant, taxi driver or tourist guide, and you can't work it out on the spot, contact your embassy or consulate for advice. Or you can go direct to the Procuraduría Federal del Consumidor (Profeco). In Mexico City the number is (55) 568-8722. There is a local Profeco office at all major destinations within

Mexico. For grievances involving people or organisations not normally associated with the tourist industry, it is recommended that you go to the local police station. In Mexico City go to the Procuraduría del Turista on Florencia 20, tel: (55) 5625-6700.

COURTESIES AND SOCIAL CUSTOMS

Mexicans are by nature and upbringing dignified and courteous. Passengers leaving a bus may say '*gracias*' (thank you) to the bus driver and receive a '*para servirle*' (at your service) in reply. If you sneeze, someone will be sure to say '*salud*', to which you reply '*gracias*'. Always address any stranger as *Señor, Joven* (young man), or *Señorita* (even older women, unless you know they are married). Liberally use *gracias, por favor* (please) and *muy amable* (very kind of you). Shaking hands on meeting and leaving is expected. Don't be surprised if the handshake is a double-action grip involving locking thumbs. Male friends often greet each other with a bear hug and back-slapping, called an *abrazo*; women will kiss each other on the cheek, and it is also common for men and women to kiss on the cheek when greeting and saying good-bye – even in business situations. Female friends may walk arm-in-arm down the street.

A Mexican's innate desire to please and to avoid the negative may lead to waiters not bringing the bill until requested, clerks not volunteering that the office will be closed the next day due to a holiday, strangers giving directions to places they've never heard of and people agreeing to things they'll never carry out and accepting invitations they won't honour. Students of these matters say that the ancient Indian belief that only the gods decide destiny survives today in an attitude of futility concerning definite plans. There may be something to this. The *mañana* stereotype, though, bears no resemblance whatsoever to the industrious artisans, farmers and factory and office workers who turn the wheels of modern Mexico.

Women should keep in mind that there is a prevalent attitude that foreign women, especially those travelling alone, are promiscuous and sexually available. The only way around eventual misunderstandings is to dress and behave conservatively and not to respond in any way to various attentions and provocations. Women should not have any trouble being served in hotels or regular bars and restaurants, but they are not admitted into local *cantinas* or *pulquerías*. In fact, in certain places even foreign men won't be allowed into the *pulquerías*. It is not an insult, just that certain social and cultural practices are still private and Mexicans intend to keep it that way.

CRIME AND SAFETY

Pickpockets operate wherever there are crowds; be alert. Never leave your passport in the hotel room. Use the hotel safe for valuables and use the chain lock on your room. Always lock your car and don't leave valuables in sight. There are occasional robberies on buses, especially in Mexico City: always have some small change ready to pay your fare (to avoid showing your wallet). Women should avoid handbags with large openings that cannot be closed securely. Taxis have been involved in several crimes in Mexico City; use only taxis arranged through a hotel or an official agency. ATMs are also trouble spots – never use one unless other people are around and you feel safe in their presence. It is probably safer to use the ATMs found in many supermarkets and large stores. The Procuraduría del Turista was created to help tourists who are victims of a crime. To contact them call (55) 5625-6700 in Mexico City. Elsewhere, dial 060 or 080 to report a crime.

I want to report a theft	**Quiero denunciar un robo**

CUSTOMS AND ENTRY REQUIREMENTS

Formalities at a border or airport are quick and simple. Instead of a visa, visitors must have a **tourist card**, obtainable on proof of citizenship from airlines serving Mexico and at border points. This free card is valid for three months and is renewable for another three, though the renewal process is somewhat time-consuming. The tourist card will be stamped on entry and you must keep it for presentation on departure. Keep your card in a safe place with your passport and other documents – if you lose it, file a report at the local tourist office to avoid delays on departure. Tourists may visit Mexico for 72 hours without a tourist card and without paying the US$15 tax if they enter at the US-Mexico border and stay within a specified zone.

Articles brought into Mexico are subject to duty and require an import permit. However, visitors are given a duty-free allowance of exempted goods as follows: 500 cigarettes or 100 cigars or 250g of tobacco; 3 litres of wine or spirits; equipment such as a camera, camcorder, portable radio, portable cassette/CD player, laptop computer (one of each per person).

I have nothing to declare	**No tengo nada que declarar**

Currency restrictions. Non-residents may import or export any amount of freely convertible foreign currency into Mexico provided it is declared on arrival. There is also no limit to the amount of Mexican currency you may carry into or out of Mexico.

D

DRIVING

Any valid driving licence is accepted in Mexico. If you bring your own car, you must present proof of ownership at the border, where it will be registered with your tourist card. Only the owner of the car can drive it; otherwise, you need to have a notarised letter stating the names of those who will be driving. Take out full accident and liability Mexican insurance at the border, since cover from most other countries does not apply. Have your car thoroughly checked before departure and bring along any spare parts such as a fan belt and oil filter, which may be difficult to obtain. A container of water and a petrol can are good insurance. Get a good road map from your automobile club (they are not sold in petrol stations); it should also describe the common road signs.

Most Mexican surfaced roads are two-lane, very winding in the mountains and often without shoulders. While the main highways are generally in good condition, be careful when rounding curves and topping rises: there may be cows or a poorly-marked hazard just out of sight; it is not uncommon to encounter a bus slowly passing an even slower vehicle. Try to avoid driving at night – traffic with no headlights abound. Rocks or branches on the road are often placed there to indicate a broken-down vehicle ahead or a huge pothole in the middle of the road. Look out for sign in villages and near schools announcing *topes* or *vibradores*. These humps are placed across the road to slow traffic; they are sometimes hard to spot, and always nasty to hit at high speed. Visitors are strongly advised to avoid driving in Mexico City if they can.

If you have car trouble, raise your bonnet and wait for the 'Green Angels' (*Ángeles Verdes*). These green government repair trucks patrol the main routes from 8am–7pm, making minor repairs and supplying emergency petrol, charging only the cost of the materials. If you have a mobile phone, you can call them at 300-26300 ext. 2950. An alternative is to flag a passing car or lorry and ask the driver to alert the Green Angels on your behalf, keeping in mind that most truck operators don't speak English.

Pemex is the federal petrol supplier, and while petrol is still distributed through the government only, some service stations are now independent concessions. The new ones usually include well-stocked convenience stores and toilets that are reasonably clean. There are two kinds of petrol, both unleaded: *magna* (83 octane) and *premium* (97 octane). Diesel is available, but not all service stations carry it. Fill up whenever your tank is half-empty: it may be a long drive to the next station. Tip service station attendants for filling the tank and other services, such as cleaning the windscreen. Credit cards are not accepted at most service stations.

Most Mexican road signs are the standard international pictographs. But you may encounter these written signs:

Aduana	Customs
Alto	Stop
Autopista (de cuota)	(Toll) highway
Camino deteriorado (en malas condiciones)	Bad road
Ceda el paso	Give way
Cruce peligroso	Dangerous crossing
Cuidado	Caution
Despacio	Slow
Desviación	Detour
Escuela	School
Peligro	Danger
Prohibido estacionarse	No parking
Prohibido (No) rebasar	No overtaking
Puesto de socorro	First-aid station
Puente angosto	Narrow bridge
Salida de camiones	Truck exit

Are we on the right road for…?	**¿Es esta la carretera hacia…?**
Fill the tank, top grade, please	**Llénelo, con premium, por favor**
Check the oil/tyres/battery, please	**Revise el aceite/las llantas/ la batería, por favor**
I've had a breakdown	**Mi carro se ha descompuesto**
There's been an accident	**Ha habido un accidente**

DRUGS

Stay away from them. For all the talk about 'Acapulco Gold', drugs are illegal and not tolerated in Mexico. If the Federal Police pick you up on suspicion of drug possession or dealing, you can be held for an extended period of time without trial – in Mexico, the underlying principle of the law is that you are assumed guilty until proven innocent. If you are charged with even possession, a jail sentence is inevitable.

ELECTRICITY

Mains electricity is 120 volts, 60 cycles; but sockets are equipped for two flat pins only. Appliances using other systems will require a transformer and/or an adapter plug. Voltage variations are very common, so it is recommended to have a surge protector and regulator.

EMBASSIES AND CONSULATES (*Embajadas/Consulados*)

Australian Embassy: Ruben Dario 55, Col. Polanco, Mexico City, CP 11580, tel: (55) 1101-2200; <www.dfat.gov.au/missions/countries/mx.html

Canadian Embassy: Schiller 529, Colonia Polanco, Mexico City, CP 11570, tel: (55) 5724-7900; <www.canada.org/mx>

New Zealand Embassy: José Luis LaGrange 103, 10th floor, Col. Polanco, Mexico City, CP 11570, tel: (55) 5283-9460

South African Embassy: Andres Bello 10, 9th floor, Col. Polanco, Mexico City, CP 11510, tel: (55) 5282-9260

UK Embassy: Rio Lerma 71, Col. Cuauhtemoc, Mexico City, CP 06500, tel: (55) 5242-8500; <www.embajadabritanica.com.mx>

US Embassy: Paseo de la Reforma 305, Col. Cuauhtemoc, Mexico City, CP 06500, tel: (55) 5080-2000; <www.usembassy-mexico.gov>

British Consulates

Centro Internacional Acapulco, Costera Miguel Alemán, Acapulco, Guerrero, CP 39851, tel: (744) 484-1735

Royal Sands, Blvd, Kukulcán Km 13.5, Cancún, Quintana Roo, CP 77500, tel: (998) 881-0100

Fresno 185, Campestre Juárez, Cd. Juárez, Chihuahua, CP 32460, tel: (614) 617-5791

Jesús de Rochas 20, Col. Los Pinos, Zapopan, Jalisco, CP 45120, tel: (33) 3343-2296

Blvd Salinas 1500, Fracc. Aviación Tijuana, Baja California Norte, CP 2240, tel: (6640) 686-5320

Ave. Ricardo Margáin Zozaya 240, 2nd Floor, Monterrey, Nuevo León, CP 66200, tel: (81) 8315-2049

Independencia 1349-1, Veracruz, Veracruz, CP 91700, tel: (229) 931-1285

Hotel Xestal, Blvd Chahuate Lote 37, Mza 4, Sector R, Bahias de Huatulco, Oaxaca, tel: (958) 587-2372

US Consulates

Progreso 175, Guadalajara, Jalisco, CP 44100, tel: (33) 3268-2100

Monterrey 141 Pte., Hermosillo, Sonora, CP 83000, tel: (662) 289-3500

Ave. Primera 2002 and Azaleas, Matamoros, Tamaulipas, CP 87330, tel: (868) 812-4402

Paseo Montejo 453, Merida, Yucatán, CP 97000, tel: (999) 925-5011

Tapachula 96, Col. Hipódromo, Tijuana, BCN, CP 22420, tel: (664) 622-7400

Hotel Acapulco Continental, Office 14, Acapulco, Guerrero, CP 39580, tel: (744) 469-0556

Blvd Marina and Pedregal #1, Local C-4, Cabo San Lucas, BCS, tel: (624) 143-3566

Plaza Caracol II, 2nd floor, Local 320-323, Blvd Kukulcán Km 8.5, Cancún, Quintana Roo, CP 77500, tel: (998) 883-0272

Hotel Fontan, Blvd Ixtapa, Ixtapa, Guerrero, CP 40880, tel: (755) 533-2100

Macedonio Alcalá 201, Office 206, Oaxaca, Oaxaca, CP 68000, tel: (951) 514-3054

Vallarta Building, Zaragoza 160, 2nd floor, Puerto Vallarta, Jalisco, CP 48300, tel: (322) 222-0069

Venustiano Carranza 2076–41, San Luis Potosí, SLP, CP 96000, tel: (441) 811-7802

Dr. Hernándeaz Macías 72, San Miguel de Allende, Guanajuato, CP 37700, tel: (415) 152-2357

G

GETTING THERE

Most international flights arrive at Mexico City airport. International airlines have direct flights into Mexico from almost every major airport in the US. There are also direct flights from London, Frankfurt, Paris, Amsterdam, Madrid, Sydney and Johannesburg (most of these operate weekly or several times a week). In many cases, European travellers to Mexico may find it more convenient to make connections in New York or another US gateway. During the high season (winter months) several airlines fly directly from the US and elsewhere into major resort areas.

GUIDES

All types of ingratiating types will offer to be helpful. If you want a guide, get one who is accredited by the Secretariat of Tourism from your hotel or a travel agency. At major museums and archaeological sites, tours by official guides are available. The more foreign tourists that visit a place, the more likely it is that you can find guides who speak foreign languages. It is customary to give tour guides a tip.

We'd like an English-speaking guide	**Queremos un guía que hable inglés**
I need an English interpreter	**Necesito un intérprete en inglés**

H

HEALTH AND MEDICAL CARE

No vaccinations are required for entry, but your doctor may recommend updating your tetanus and polio immunisation and suggest a vaccination as a hepatitis deterrent. Mexico City and many other towns are above 1,300m (7,000ft), an altitude that will affect some visitors more than others. If you notice shortness of breath, a slight headache and a tired feeling, take it easy on exercise, food and drink for the first day or two and the symptoms will disappear. Along with the altitude, in Mexico City the pollution will probably also affect the way you feel – breathing the air on an average day is said to be the equivalent to smoking 40 cigarettes. On some days you may not notice it; on others it will make your nose run and your eyes water.

The most notorious Mexican health hazard, variously known to tourists as the *turista* or 'Moctezuma's Revenge', is a relatively harmless combination of diarrhoea and upset stomach that travellers encounter worldwide. It is caused mostly by the different chemicals and bacteria encountered in the water. The best way to avoid this nuisance is to refrain from drinking tap water, consume only purified bottled water, and take ice only in places where you are quite sure that it is made from purified water, such as in restaurants that cater for tourists. The machine-made ice cubes in first-class establishments are usually safe, but usually doesn't mean always – you can always ask for drinks *sin hielo* (without ice). It is hard to pass up the delicious fruits and juices in markets or the savoury snacks offered at street stands, but it is best to play it safe until you've been in the country for a couple of weeks and have made peace with the unfamiliar local bacteria.

a bottle of mineral water	**una botella de agua mineral**
carbonated/non-carbonated	**con gas/sin gas**

If you do succumb, take plenty of liquids, such as herbal tea like *manzanilla* (camomile) with a little salt (a pinch) and sugar (a tea-spoon), or sports drinks like Gatorade that will replenish some of the minerals you lose. Mexican pharmacies sell most drugs without prescription and are familiar with proven local remedies for *turista*. In almost every tourist destination there are chemists that open 24 hours, and even deliver without an extra charge. Otherwise, there are chemists that take it in turns to remain open after hours and at weekends. Your hotel will tell you the location of the *farmacia de turno*.

In an emergency, most first-class hotels have a doctor on call who will speak English and other foreign languages. Embassies and consulates also have a list of multilingual doctors. A couple of hospitals with bilingual staff are: American-British Cowdray (ABC) Hospital, Calle Sur 132 136, Colonia Las Américas, Mexico City, tel: (55) 5230-8000; and Mexico-Americano Hospital, Colomos 2110, Guadalajara, Jalisco, tel: (33) 3641-3625/ 3641-3141.

Get me a doctor, quickly!	**¡Llamen a un médico, rápido!**

HOLIDAYS *(Días Festivos)*

The Mexican fiesta calendar offers a full array of celebrations to choose from. There are states that seem to have a celebration, religious, political or otherwise, almost every day of the year. But apart from regional fiestas, there are 13 official holidays when all public offices, museums, banks, etc are closed:

1 January	*Año Nuevo*	New Year's Day
5 February	*Aniversario de la Constitución*	Constitution Day
21 March	*Nacimiento de Benito Juárez*	Benito Juárez's Birthday

1 May	*Día del Trabajo*	Labour Day
5 May	*Batalla de Puebla*	Anniversary of the Battle of Puebla
1 September	*Informe Presidencial*	First day of Congress
16 September	*Día de la Independencia*	Independence Day
12 October	*Día de la Raza*	Columbus Day, 'Day of the Race'
2 November	*Día de los Muertos*	All Souls' Day
20 November	*Aniversario de la Revolución*	Anniversary of the Revolution
12 December	*Nuestra Señora de Guadalupe*	Our Lady of Guadalupe
25 December	*Navidad*	Christmas Day
Movable dates	*Pascua, Semana Santa*	Easter, Holy Week

L

LANGUAGE

Mexico is the largest Spanish-speaking country in the world. In addition, Mexican Indians speak 58 indigenous languages or dialects, with Spanish as their *lingua franca*. English is understood in hotels and tourist-oriented establishments throughout the country – even Indian women in the market may be able to quote prices in English. Official guides qualified in foreign languages may be engaged through travel agencies or located through local tourism offices. But any Spanish you possess or phrases you learn will be appreciated by Mexicans and will make asking directions, shopping and ordering food easier.

Remember – you are a visitor in this country and locals serve you a courtesy by speaking, or trying to speak, your language. The least you can try to do is return the courtesy by trying to speak some phrases in Spanish, or at least not get frustrated if somebody doesn't speak English.

Some useful vocabulary

Yes/no	**Sí/no**
Please/thank you	**Por favor/gracias**
Excuse me/you're welcome	**Perdón/de nada**
Where/when/how	**Dónde/cuándo/cómo**
How long/how far	**Cuánto tiempo/qué distancia**
Left/right	**Izquierda/derecha**
Good/bad	**Bueno/malo**
Big/small	**Grande/pequeño**
Cheap/expensive	**Barato/caro**
Hot/cold	**Caliente/frío**
Old/new	**Viejo/nuevo**
Open/closed	**Abierto/cerrado**
Do you speak English?	**¿Habla inglés?**
I don't understand	**No entiendo**
Please write it down	**Escríbalo, por favor**
Help me please	**Ayúdeme, por favor**
I'd like…	**Quisiera…**
What time is it?	**¿Qué hora es?**

Numbers

1	**uno**	11	**once**	40	**cuarenta**
2	**dos**	12	**doce**	50	**cincuenta**
3	**tres**	13	**trece**	60	**sesenta**
4	**cuatro**	14	**catorce**	70	**setenta**
5	**cinco**	15	**quince**	80	**ochenta**
6	**seis**	16	**dieciséis**	90	**noventa**
7	**siete**	17	**diecisiete**	100	**cien**
8	**ocho**	20	**veinte**	101	**ciento uno**
9	**nueve**	21	**veintiuno**	500	**quinientos**
10	**diez**	30	**treinta**	1,000	**mil**

Days and months			
Sunday	**domingo**	January	**enero**
Monday	**lunes**	February	**febrero**
Tuesday	**martes**	March	**marzo**
Wednesday	**miércoles**	April	**abril**
Thursday	**jueves**	May	**mayo**
Friday	**viernes**	June	**junio**
Saturday	**sábado**	July	**julio**
yesterday	**ayer**	August	**agosto**
today	**hoy**	September	**septiembre**
tomorrow	**mañana**	October	**octubre**
day/week/month/year		November	**noviembre**
día/semana/mes/año		December	**diciembre**

LOST PROPERTY

Every state and major city of Mexico has a Tourist Department with a telephone number for tourist assistance (see TOURIST INFORMATION). If your hotel can't solve your problem, ask someone to contact this number or the local Policía Judicial for you. In Mexico City report lost property to the Procuraduría del Turista on (55) 5625-6700. It is especially important to report a lost passport or other personal documents.

The Procuraduría Federal de la Nación offers a nationwide service to locate missing persons and lost property. To make a report or an inquiry contact them on (55) 568-8722. Locatel in Mexico City offers a computerised telephone service, which provides information about missing persons and stolen vehicles. Phone them on (55) 658-1111.

I've lost my wallet/ handbag/passport	**He perdido mi cartera/ bolsa/pasaporte**

M

MEDIA

A considerable number of daily newspapers are published in Mexico City, most of them heavily oriented towards local and national events. Only in the leading hotels and bookstores of the main cities will you find foreign newspapers. Foreign magazines are easier to find, since they are usually available in drugstores and tobacconists at hotels and airports. While you can occasionally find European and even a few Asian publications, it is more common to find US newspapers and magazines.

For those who are interested in staying up to date with the international news, sometimes it is easier to do it through television, since most hotels offer either cable or satellite TV with at least one US channel that broadcasts current news.

There are several radio stations that play music in Spanish and English all day. On Saturdays and Sundays at 10am, Imagen (90.5FM) broadcasts the English-language news programme *Living in Mexico*, covering economics, politics and sport.

Have you any magazines/ newspapers in English?	**¿Tiene revistas/ periódicos en inglés?**

MEETING PEOPLE

Mexicans are exceptionally friendly people, though you must first overcome their initial reserve. This can be accomplished swiftly by a smile and a question or remark in Spanish. If someone recognises your accent and can speak your language they will be delighted to demonstrate it.

Mexican women follow rigid codes of behaviour and may not respond if you misinterpret your interest. On the other hand, men who approach you – usually on the street and often asking, 'Where are you from?' – are most likely hustlers. When you are out for a night in the town, it is important to remember that while Mexican men are friendly and love to have fun, they are also very jealous of their girlfriends, sisters and any other female acquaintance that may be part of the group. So it is important to act in a polite and courteous manner.

MONEY

The currency of Mexico is the **peso**, designated by the international currency sign $ (in this book we have not used the $ sign for prices, to avoid confusion with the US$). A peso is divided into 100 centavos, but you will only find 10, 20 and 50 centavo coins, and usually prices are rounded to the closest peso amount, so instead of something being 1.50 (one peso and fifty centavos) it will be 2 pesos. There are also coins worth 1, 5, 10 and 20 pesos. Bills are issued in 20, 50, 100, 200 and 500 pesos. The bills come in different sizes and colours. Be careful not to accept bills that are torn, ripped, taped or otherwise damaged, as neither businesses nor banks will accept them.

Banking hours. Banks are normally open Monday–Friday 9am–3pm. Increasingly, banks are extending their hours until 5 or 7pm and some are now open on Saturday 10am–2pm. Most banks will exchange foreign currency during banking hours. Keep in mind that banks are usually crowded on the first, 15th and last day of the month, because these are paydays for most employees. Fridays are especially busy days for all banks.

Changing money. There is no black market and the peso fluctuates daily a tiny bit, a good reason for not cashing too much currency at one time. All banks offer the same rate as it is published daily in Mexico City and broadcast to all banks. Some banks charge a 1 percent fee to exchange travellers' cheques, and you will need your passport as ID. Private Exchange Houses (Casas de Cambio) will change currency and travellers' cheques at or near bank rates, and are open longer hours and on many holidays. Try to keep small change in pesos, such as 5 and 10 peso coins, for tipping, paying taxis and small purchases. Merchants and drivers frequently can't (or won't) give change. Hotels will exchange money at all hours, but at less favourable rates.

ATMs. Many banks now have cash machines where you can withdraw funds from your bank account or credit card in pesos, and usually at a favourable exchange rate. However, be extremely cautious when using these machines, especially in Mexico City and other large cities. Try to use them in well-populated areas only during daylight hours, or seek out the ATMs in supermarkets and Sanborns stores.

Credit cards. Leading credit cards are widely accepted throughout Mexico, though not in most petrol stations. If you are planning to charge a hotel bill or a meal, it is advisable to ask which credit cards are accepted by the establishment. Most hotels, restaurants and shops in resort areas will take travellers' cheques. US dollars are widely accepted in resort areas, airports and border towns, and sometimes the prices are even quoted in dollars.

I want to change some dollars/pounds.	**Quiero cambiar dólares/libras esterlinas**
Do you accept travellers' cheques?	**¿Acepta cheques de viajero?**
Can I pay with this credit card?	**¿Puedo pagar con esta tarjeta de crédito?**
How much?	**¿Cuánto es?**
Have you anything cheaper?	**¿Tiene algo más barato?**

O

OPENING HOURS

In the capital and major cities, shops and offices open at 9 or 10am and remain open until 6pm or even later. In most resorts and in cities in the interior of Mexico, shops and offices usually close from 2 until 4 and then remain open until 7 or 8pm.

Museums vary in their opening hours (*see Where to Go section*) but are usually closed on Mondays. Banks have traditionally been open 9am–3pm; however, more and more banks are modernising and, in the process, extending their office hours until 5, 6 or 7pm. Some are also opening on Saturdays 10am–2pm. As a rule, the larger the city, the longer the business hours. Sunday is still the universal day-off in Mexico, when most offices and shops are closed.

Are you open tomorrow?	**¿Está abierto mañana?**

P

PHOTOGRAPHY

Well-known brands of film are widely available in all varieties. Processing can be done in an hour in most cities and resort areas, and there are overnight or two-day developing places all over Mexico. However, slides (*diapositivas*) do take longer, up to a week, and only certain labs offer that service, so you are better off sticking to prints. Videocassettes are also in good supply; however, while pre-made videos are compatible with systems in the US, they will not run on many European systems.

Remember that the sun is very bright in the coastal areas. You won't need high-speed film for most purposes, but the use of a flash is restricted in many artistic and archaeological sites. In quite a few museums, tourist sites and churches you may have to check your camera at the entrance or pay a fee to use it. Also, remember that many people – especially Indian communities in thr more remote areas – do not like to have their pictures taken and you must respect their wishes.

I'd like a film for this camera	**Quisiera un rollo para esta cámara**
...for colour pictures	**...para fotografía en color**
...for black and white	**...en blanco y negro**
...for colour slides	**...para transparencias**
35-mm film	**treinta y cinco milímetros**
How long will it take to develop (and print) this film?	**¿Cuánto tardará en revelar (e imprimir) este rollo?**
May I take a picture?	**¿Puedo tomar una foto?**

POLICE *(Policía)*

There are several branches of the police in Mexico. The local or municipal police are the ones who intervene in case of a mishap in any public area such as parks, restaurants, bars, etc. There is also a traffic division, in charge of all traffic-related incidents. Then there are the State, Federal and Judicial police. Each force has different jurisdictions, but in case of an incident where police intervention is needed, any passing patrol, regardless of their jurisdiction, will offer assistance.

The Ministerio Público is the division in charge of crimes and the office you need to report to in case of a robbery or assault. In Mexico City, you can call the bilingual staff at the Procuraduría del Turista, tel: (55) 5625-6700, in case of an incident that you need to report. Everywhere in Mexico, you can dial 060 or 080 for police assistance in case of an emergency, but operators generally do not speak English.

POST OFFICES (*Correos*)

Post offices are usually open Monday–Friday 9am–6pm and Saturday 9am–1pm.

General delivery (*Lista de correos*). If you plan an extended stay in any one place but you don't know in advance where you'll be staying, you can have your mail addressed to the *Lista de Correos* in any town. The office will hold the mail for ten days before returning it.

Postboxes/mailboxes (*Buzones*). If you have a choice of slots, always put international mail in the one marked *Aéreo* (air mail); *Terrestre* is for surface mail.

Have you any mail for…?	**¿Tiene correo para…?**
stamp/letter/postcard	**timbre/carta/tarjeta postal**
special delivery (express)	**urgente**
airmail	**correo aéreo**
registered	**correo certificado**

PUBLIC TRANSPORT

By air. Internal air travel is the most efficient way to travel around the country. Fares are relatively low and you'll avoid time-consuming and tiresome bus or train trips; even if you don't make arrangements before arriving in Mexico, you can check with any local travel agent for schedules and fares.

By bus. In town and between cities, the average Mexican prefers to travel by bus. Without a doubt the bus system is the cheapest, most practical way to travel around town and around the country. For in-town service, routes usually run along the main streets. Mexico City's newest tourist service is the *Turibus*, red open-topped double-decker buses that circulate 9am–10pm, linking many of the museums and popular sites. A daily pass entitles you to hop on and off at will. To travel between towns and cities, most travellers prefer the deluxe and first-class buses. Tickets are usually sold at the bus terminal or through a local travel agent. The most accurate source of information about rates and schedule is the station itself. Be aware that first-class and second-class bus services usually operate from different bus stations: for first-class, seek out the Central de Autobuses (or Camiones) de Primer Clase. When planning to travel by bus, check the schedules and, to ensure a seat, buy your ticket the day before the trip, or at least early in the day of the trip.

What's the fare to…?	¿Cuál es la tarifa a…?

By train. There is no passenger train service in Mexico with the exception of the Copper Canyon route (*see page 128*), a single-track line serviced by a deluxe train that runs between Los Mochis in Sinaloa state and Chihuahua City (14 hours).

Taxis. Taxis are normally not expensive, but if you are in a place where taxis don't have meters, you should definitely ask the driver how much the ride will cost before starting out. In Mexico City *do not hail a passing taxi in the street*. Several crimes involving taxis have occurred in the green VW-mini taxis. Most hotels have official taxi drivers who are regulated by the union and city.

Another 'safe' taxi option is to use an authorised, or *sitio*, **taxi base**; hotels and restaurants can call these radio-dispatched taxis for you. Official Radio Taxis, tel: (55) 5271-9146, (55) 5271-9058 or (55) 5272-6125, are also considered safe. You can hire one of these taxis from your hotel; the driver will frequently act as your personal driver and escort you through your travels in the city. This is a particularly advisable option at night. The average rate for this service is around 100 pesos per hour.

R

RELIGION

Mexico is predominantly Catholic. However, there are Protestant churches in most cities. Churches in larger cities and resort areas often have Sunday services in English. In major cities services are held in synagogues in both Spanish and Hebrew.

What time is mass/ the service?	**¿A qué hora es la misa/ el servicio?**
Is it in English?	**¿Es en inglés?**

T

TELEPHONES

Public phones operated by Telmex are in grey booths marked 'Ladatel'. They are abundant and offer the cheapest calling options. They operate with Ladatel debit cards, which can be purchased in drugstores and convenience stores in denominations of 30, 50 and 100 pesos. You can also find coin-operated public phones in stores and pharmacies, but less frequently. Usually the first minute of any local call costs 2 pesos. If you are going to use a coin-operated phone, make sure that you have plenty of 2 peso coins. If you put a 5 or 10 peso coin in the phone and you don't use up all the time you will not get change.

Long Distance Dialling: within Mexico, dial 01; to call the US or Canada, dial 001. Dial 090 from any phone to make a reverse-charge (collect) call. As a rule, long-distance calls are very expensive. Hotels charge extra for long-distance calls and you are better off calling collect. You can also use the services offered by *casetas*. They offer operator-placed phone calls and usually also have fax service; some provide Internet connections. While the smaller, more remote towns inside Mexico may only have a *caseta* and no public phones, these types of services are usually more expensive that the Ladatel option.

All over Mexico, dial 040 (information, directory assistance), 060 and 080 (police/emergency), 090 (international operator) and 020 (national operator). Remember that directory assistance will only work if you have the exact name under which a phone is registered; for example, the small hotel you know as El Escondite might be registered under the owner's name and there will be no listing for El Escondite. Most Mexican telephone numbers consist of a three-digit area code, followed by a seven-digit number. The exception is Mexico City, where the area code 55 is followed by an eight-digit number. The national code for calling Mexico from overseas is 52.

Can you get me this number?	**¿Puede comunicarme con este número?**
Reverse-charge (collect) call	**por cobrar**
Person-to-person (personal) call	**de persona a persona**
I want to send a telegram to…	**Quiero mandar un telegrama…**

TIME ZONES

Most of Mexico is on Central Standard Time (GMT minus 6 hours). The states of Baja California Sur, Nayarit, Sinaloa and Sonora are on Mountain Standard Time (GMT minus 7 hours). Baja California Norte is on Pacific Standard Time (GMT minus 8 hours). The country observes Daylight Savings Time (clocks one hour forward from the first Sunday in April to the last in October).

What time is it?	**¿Qué hora es?**

TIPPING

Wages are low in Mexico and most service-oriented employees count on tips to make up the majority of their income. This is especially true for bellboys and waiters. Bellboys receive 5 to 10 pesos per bag; waiters generally receive 10 to 20 percent of the bill, depending on the level of service; some restaurants include the tip in the bill – especially when serving large parties – so check your bill to make sure. Maids receive between 50 and 100 pesos per week, depending on the service. In Mexico, it is not customary to tip taxi drivers, unless they are hired by the hour, or provide touring or other special services. Keep a supply of coins handy for the inevitable tip.

Keep the change	**Es para usted**

TOILETS

In Mexico the toilets may be referred to as *baños*, *sanitarios*, *tocadores*, *escusados* or *WC*. The doors may be labelled *caballeros* or *H* (*hombres*) for men and *M* (*mujeres*) or *damas* for women. Progress has been made recently in keeping public toilets clean, but always carry tissues with you. Usually you have to pay 1 or 2 pesos to get some toilet paper; and an attendant who hands you towels expects a small tip.

Where are the toilets?	**¿Dónde están los baños?**

TOURIST OFFICES (*Oficinas de turismo*)

The Mexican government maintains many tourist offices abroad, and any Mexican consulate will provide information about travel to Mexico. Here is a list of some Mexican Government Tourist Offices:

UK: Wakefield House, 41 Trinity Square, London EC3N 4DJ, tel: (020) 7488-9392

US: Toll Free: 1-800-44 mexico
300 N. Michigan Ave., Chicago, IL 60601, tel: (312) 606-9252
1200 N.W. 78th Ave., Suite 203, Miami, FL 33126; tel. (305) 718-4091
21 E. 63rd St., 2nd floor, New York, NY 10021; tel. (212) 821-0314
Canada: 1 Place Ville-Marie, Suite 1931, Montréal, QUEB, H3B 2C3, tel: (514) 871-1052
2 Bloor St. W., Suite 1502, Toronto, ON, M4W 3E2, tel: (416) 925-2753

You can get a list of the local Tourist Offices in the places you plan to visit by calling SECTUR in Mexico City, tel: (55) 5250-0123. The best source of tourist information is Infotur, a SECTUR that provides bilingual tourist information about attractions, transport, accommodation and anything else you might need. The toll-free number inside Mexico is 800-903-9200; their number in Mexico City is (55) 5250-0123. The Mexican Tourist Board has a comprehensive website <www.visitmexico.com>.

Where is the nearest tourist office?	**¿Dónde está la oficina de turismo más cercana?**

W

WEIGHTS AND MEASURES

Mexico uses the metric system.

Y

YOUTH HOSTELS (*Albergues de la juventud*)

Mexico has a network of youth hostels with more than 300 participating hotels and hostels. For information, contact Instituto Mexicano de la Juventud – Turismo Juvenil, Serapio Rendón 76, Col. San Rafael, México, DF, CP 06470, or visit <www.hostelweb.com/cities/mexicocity.html>

INDEX